Y0-CCS-960

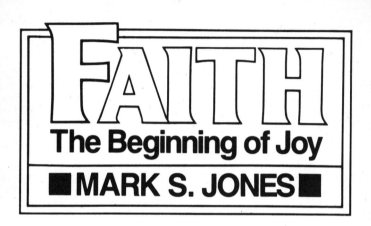

FAITH
The Beginning of Joy
■ MARK S. JONES ■

BROADMAN PRESS
Nashville, Tennessee

© Copyright 1989 • Broadman Press

All rights reserved

4257-37

ISBN: 0-8054-5737-2

Dewey Decimal Classification: 234.2

Subject Heading: CHRISTIAN LIFE // FAITH

Library of Congress Catalog Card Number: 89-31009

Printed in the United States of America

Unless otherwise noted, Scripture quotations are from the HOLY BIBLE *New International Version,* copyright © 1978, New York Bible Society. Used by permission. Scripture quotations marked (KJV) are from the King James Version of the Bible. Scripture quotations marked (RSV) are from the Revised Standard Version of the Bible, copyrighted 1946, 1952, © 1971, 1973.

Library of Congress Cataloging-in-Publication Data

Jones, Mark S., 1954-
    Faith: the beginning of joy / Mark S. Jones.
        p. cm.
    ISBN 0-8054-5737-2
    1. Consolation.   2. Faith.   3. Christian life—1960-   I. Title.
    BV4905.2.J67   1989   89-31009
    248.4—dc19   CIP

Preface

> During the days of Jesus' life on earth, he offered up prayers and petitions with loud cries and tears to the one who could save him from death, and he was heard because of his reverent submission. Although he was a son, he learned obedience from what he suffered and, once made perfect, he became the source of eternal salvation for all who obey him and was designated by God to be high priest in the order of Melchizedek (Heb. 5:7-10).

Who can fathom the darkness of the human soul? After years of pastoral ministry I still look with mystery into the painful possibilities which lie inside the hearts and souls of persons, not to think of my own abyss. Jesus must have measured the depths of human agony during His hours on the cross. "My God, my God, why have you forsaken me?" are the words of desperate pain echoing from the cries of the psalmist, reiterated from Calvary, reverberating in the hearts of every person who has lived and loved.

The Scriptures say that Jesus "for the joy set before him endured the cross" (Heb. 12:2). Ministry could be defined as helping people see the joy set before them so that they may endure the crucibles of life. That's where faith comes in. "Now faith is being sure of what we hope for and certain of what we do not see" (Heb. 11:1).

Faith has a transforming quality. Circumstances can be transformed, and perspectives can be lifted to new vistas. This is a book about the transforming power of faith in the midst of life's dramas. It is for any Christian who welcomes an interpretation of the Christian life from a different perspective. It is for ministers who seek fresh insight into effective ministry (as well as fodder for sermons). It is for leaders in the church, lay as well as clergy, who help those who help others—who minister to the ministers and encourage the encouragers.

It is a book about real life—from which even the Christian is not immune—that can be faced with a contagious faith. It is a book for those looking for answers to life's perplexities from a perplexed seeker. It is a journey we'll walk together.

Contents

Introduction

How to Have Joy? You Must Be Joking!

I have told you this so that my joy may be in you and that your joy may be complete (John 15:11).

A young pastor eagerly moved into his first full-time pastorate. As he was moving into his new study and arranging things in his desk, he discovered a large envelope left by the previous pastor. On the front it said, "How to Pastor This Church." The puzzled minister opened the mysterious envelope only to discover three smaller envelopes, each marked with a number. On the first envelope was written, "Open when the first major crisis comes." The other two envelopes were for the second and third crises. The preacher slid the envelopes back into the bottom drawer and soon forgot about them.

After about six months, things were not going well for the new pastor. In fact, rumor had it that the deacons were discussing whether to ask him to resign. Just then, the pastor remembered the three envelopes. Rushing to his study, he opened envelope one. "Blame me" was all it said. So the next Sunday the pastor preached his sermon and said, "All our problems in this church are the result of the last pastor." It seemed to suit the people fine, and soon things were on an even keel again.

When the next major crisis came, the pastor opened the second envelope. "Blame the denomination" was its message. On the next Sunday, the members heard a scathing denunciation of the denomination's programs and how they were the cause of all the church's problems. It worked.

Before long, the tide turned again, and the young pastor confidently opened the third envelope. It read, "Prepare three envelopes."

I'm sure many of us wish we had three envelopes to help us get through the struggles of life. We would like to believe that the solutions to life's intricate problems could be simple. But, by blindly following a series of simplistic solutions, we are ever doomed to struggle with the real and complicated issues. Sometimes I feel like the man in the old folk song, "There's a Hole in My Bucket."

> There's a hole in my bucket, dear Liza, dear Liza.
> Mend the hole then, dear Willie, you silly, mend it.
> With what shall I mend it . . . ?
> With a straw then . . .
> But the straw is too long . . .
> Cut the straw then . . .
> With what shall I cut it . . . ?
> With a knife then . . .
> But the knife is too dull . . .
> Whet the knife then . . .
> With what will I whet it . . . ?
> With a stone then . . .
> But the stone is too rough . . .
> Smooth the stone then . . .
> With what shall I smooth it . . . ?
> With water . . .
> In what shall I carry it . . . ?
> In a bucket . . . !
> But, there's a hole in my bucket . . . !

It is frustrating to discover that the solution to one problem only forms the basis of another problem. In the midst of the confusion and frustration it is easy to lose joy, to become bitter and sour at life.

People come by our church office from time to time seeking assistance with "financial problems." Some are chronic users of benevolent aid. They see their problem as a series of simple solutions: a gas voucher today, a bag of groceries tomorrow, food stamps on Wednesday, and rent assistance once a month. Never do they seem to realize the pattern of their lives. As long as they can convince themselves the "problem" is that Lady Luck has dealt them a bad hand, or that circumstances have temporarily turned against them, they will remain blind to the real issue: irresponsibility.[1]

We must take responsibility for our actions and our *attitudes.* Attitudes are simply the result of willful decisions. When taking a morning walk, I often pass a neighbor who is *always* exuberant with happiness. He sings and smiles and walks with a spark in his gait. He will talk your ear off if you linger. I, on the other hand, walk down the street preoccupied with the stresses of ministry. In conversation my neighbor belies any Christian or religious commitment. Why is he so happy? *Because he has decided to be happy!* I decide some mornings to be preoccupied with the stresses of ministry!

What is your basic attitude about life? As a starting point for looking at your attitude, try taking this "State of Your Life Quiz":

State of Your Life Quiz

_____1. Can you say that life is worth living?
    Indisputably yes=10; sort of=5; no=0

_____2. Are you pleased with where you are in life now?
    Yes=10; no=0

_____3. When was the last time you really enjoyed yourself?
    Recently=10; long time=5; can't remember=0

_____4. Do you feel that your life has real meaning?
    Yes=10; fuzzy=5; don't know what you mean=0

_____5. Do you feel that your life is a blessing to others?
    To most people=10; some=5; few or none=0

_____6. When you go to bed at night, do you often feel a sense of accomplishment or satisfaction with the day?=10;
    Or, do you often find yourself being preoccupied with tomorrow or yesterday?=0

_____7. When are the "good ol' days" in your life?
    Now or recently=10; been a while=5; long time ago, or never had any=0

_____8. Do you have a plan for your life?
    Yes=10 (unless it is suicide); I've been planning to come up with one=5; no=0

_____9. Are the things you really want in life out of reach?
    No=10; no, but I have to stretch pretty hard=5; yes=0

_____10. Are you on speaking terms with God?
    Yes=10; only when I initiate the conversation=5; no=0

_____ Total

Score:
    100: You should be writing this book!
  80 - 99: An optimist
  50 - 79: A realist
  10 - 49: A pessimist

0 - 9: You need professional help

Some would debate whether a Christian should be an optimist, pessimist, or realist. Some Christians are pessimistic, with their negative view of the world and human nature. They tend to emphasize negative prophecies about a negative trend in human history—all pointing to a negative disaster of sorts. They tend to see the negative side of things. People should be held in suspicion until they prove trustworthy, they feel. Sometimes a great many stressful situations and tragic events can cause us to adopt a negative view of things too.

Christian realists want what works—practical solutions—for a world that doesn't always fit the molds of theory. Reinhold Neibuhr was a "realistic" Christian ethicist who taught that sometimes "moral men have to play hardball."[2] To Neibuhr goes credit for advancing the phrase, "the lesser of two evils." That's the stance of the realist: "Don't piddle with trying to decide what is ideal, just do the best with what you've got!" "Things are never really bad or perfect," says the realist; "you just have to take things as they come."

I must confess here and now my conviction that faith, in time, makes the Christian an incurable optimist. I just can't see it any other way. Sure, I get discouraged. I'm also very practical. But I hold an unwavering trust that things are all going to work out for the best—eventually.

Before you write me off as just another advocate of PMA (Positive Mental Attitude), hear me out. After all, what is one to do, develop a "Negative Mental Attitude"? Sure, the Christian is biblically informed about the dark side of human nature (perhaps more keenly so). The difference is that we have a cure for the spiritual diseases of humankind. Isn't that why the message of Christ is called the good news?

I'm not saying you are not a Christian if you scored below eighty on the "State of Your Life Quiz." But, certainly, there is room for improvement and the development of a more positive outlook. After all, why shouldn't the Christian be optimistic? I know the Bible has a lot of negative things to say about the world and humanity. But Christ is the crucial change-agent!

Without Christ we would rightly be pessimists. As Paul said in 1 Corinthians 15:19, "If only for this life we have hope in Christ, we are to be pitied more than all men." If it were not for Christ, the best philosophy of life would be, "Eat, drink, and be merry, for tomorrow we die." However, the same Bible that informs us of all the negative stuff of sin—judgment and damnation—also tells us: "Whatever is true, whatever is noble, whatever is right, whatever is pure, whatever is lovely, whatever is admirable—if anything is excellent or praiseworthy—think about such things" (Phil. 4:8).

Sounds pretty optimistic to me! Why cloud our thoughts with negatives all the time? The scriptural injunction is to fill our thoughts with good things! In this way we fill our lives with positive attitudes and—ultimately—positive action. "But the things that come out of the mouth come from the heart," Jesus said in Matthew 15:18. As you think, so you act.

When you first saw the title of this chapter—"How to Have Joy"— you may have responded, "You must be joking!" It sounds almost superficial. There are many superficial answers floating around these days to the joy question: "How to have joy? Get *things* that bring joy!" "How to have joy? Associate with joyful *people,* and it will rub off on you!" "How to have joy? Have *joyful thoughts!* It's simple!"

But it's not so simple. Prized material possessions bring a temporary happiness. After a while, superficially happy people just make you feel worse. And all the mind games can leave you mentally rearranged! There has to be a straight answer!

There is a biblical answer to the joy question: *God wants His children to have joy!* In John 15 Jesus spoke to His disciples about joy. He said, "I have told you this so that my joy may be in you and that your joy may be complete" (v. 11). Jesus wants every Christian to have (1) His joy and (2) complete joy.

When you think of the context of John 15—the night before Jesus was crucified—it seems rather ironic that He would talk of joy. That's the point! We can have joy while facing even the most trying situations! How can we have that kind of joy? The biblical formula for joy has at least three ingredients.

Relationships

First, there must be *positive relationships.* In John 15 Jesus spoke much about relationships. He said, "I am the vine; you are the branches. If a man remains in me and I in him, he will bear much fruit; apart from me you can do nothing" (v. 5). Jesus was touching upon the very heart of the issue: relationships. Relationships are foundational, for our values grow out of our relationships. If our relationships are positive, with the right kind of people, then our values will be positive. For example, in 1 Corinthians 15:33 Paul wrote, "Do not be misled: 'Bad company corrupts good character.' " Paul was saying, in effect, that negative relationships produce negative values.

The first four of the Ten Commandments concern the relationship of God with His people. The remaining Commandments deal with our relationships with others.

The Book of Proverbs teaches the importance of positive relationships and the need to avoid negative relationships. "Do not envy wicked men,/do not desire their company" (24:1). "He who walks with the wise grows wise,/but a companion of fools suffers harm" (13:20).

One of Paul's favorite terms was a relational proposition: "in Christ." In 2 Corinthians 5:17 Paul said, "Therefore, if anyone is *in Christ,* he is a new creation" (emphasis mine). Paul used this phrase in one form or another some two hundred times. Archibald Hunter explained the relational significance of the phrase this way:

> We must say then that the phrase means not only "in communion with Christ" but also "in the community of Christ." It describes a shared life, a *koinonia.* . . .
>
> Being "in Christ" is therefore a social experience. What Paul has in mind is changed men and women living in a changed society, with Christ the author of the change in the individual, and Christ the living centre of the new environment in which they live.[3]

What is the central relationship of your life? Out of this relationship your most fundamental values will flow. To be "in Christ" is to have your life centered in Christ and Christ centered in your life. This is not to say that Christ is just to be first in priority, but He must be central in all the relationships of life. All of life is, thus, redefined by Christ, the Center. All relationships form as concentric circles around the central relationship in Christ. Our relationship with self is redefined. We can begin to think positively about ourselves—not that we are perfect, but that we are loved and that the character of Christ is being worked out in us.

Our relationship with our spouse is redefined in light of Christ. This is exactly what Paul did in Ephesians 5. In verse 21, he began, "Submit to one another *out of reverence for Christ*" (emphasis mine). He continued, "Wives, submit to your husbands as to the Lord" (v. 22).

Then the mutual submission in Christ is defined for husbands, "Love your wives, just as Christ loved the church" (v. 25).

Our relationships with others are redefined by Jesus' command in John 15:12, "Love each other *as I have loved you*" (emphasis mine). The joy of the Christian life flows from our relationship with Christ and our relationships with others *in Christ*.

You may be wondering, *If it is so important to maintain positive relationships, then how am I supposed to win lost persons to Christ?* It is true that we must be a "friend of sinners" as Jesus was. In fact, Jesus was rejected by the religious establishment because of His willingness to befriend such "low life" as tax collectors and prostitutes. This was because Jesus did not see people as tax collectors or prostitutes, but as persons loved by God. Jesus always maintained that vital relationship with the Father *out of which* He was able to properly relate to others, even sinners.

Negative relationships occur when we allow others to assume positions of influence in our lives that belong rightly only to Christ and others of high values. When the low values of others are being transmitted into our lives, rather than our witness affecting them, our relationships have become negative. Maintaining positive relationships with others requires a constant abiding relationship in Christ.

Scratch My Back

A second biblical ingredient in the joy recipe is *positive reciprocity*. Reciprocity is the outgrowth of relationships. *Reciprocity* is a word commonly used in the diplomatic relations between countries. There is reciprocity between nations if there is a mutual benefit, such as trade. Of course, *reciprocity* can be negative, as when one country sanctions another for some intolerable action.

Both positive and negative reciprocity occur in human relationships. It's called, "Scratch my back, and I'll scratch yours." If you do me a favor, I'll return the favor. Conversely, if you exploit me, I'll exploit you. Retaliation is a common, but unchristian form of reciprocity. Jesus said, "You have heard that it was said, 'Love your neighbor and hate your enemy.' But I tell you: Love your enemies and pray for those who persecute you, that you may be sons of your Father in heaven" (Matt. 5:43-45).

Here again, positive reciprocity should be measured by Christ's definition, "Love each other as I have loved you." This is the true dynamic of the Christian community: mutual Christ-like love. This kind of reciprocity is described in Paul's admonition to the Colossians: "Let the word of Christ dwell in you richly as you teach and admonish one another with all wisdom, and as you sing psalms, hymns and spiritual songs with gratitude in your hearts to God" (Col. 3:16-17). In such an environment of love and positive relationships true Christian values can be formed. This is so crucial, since it is out of these values that actions will result.

A Christian's growth in value development goes through observable stages. We must all start school in the first grade. Likewise, we progress through these stages in our spiritual and moral growth as well, beginning at the most rudimentary level.[4]

The Eden Stage

The first stage of value development is what I also call the fear-of-retribution stage. In the earliest years of life, a person understands right and wrong in terms of what is punished and what is rewarded. "Bad" behavior is that which is punished or results in negative consequences. "Good" behavior is that which is rewarded or results in positive consequences. For example, when the three-year-old draws on the wall with a crayon, punishment may soon result. However, when the child draws a picture in the coloring book, he or she may receive all manner of compliments. Therefore, the rationale for behavior becomes the avoidance of retribution or the attainment of reward.

Fear is the operative word in this stage. If I don't do what I am supposed to do, or if I do that which I am not supposed to do, I will receive retribution. This is the moral world of the child. Reciprocity is understood in the simplest of terms: If I do good, good things will result; but if I do bad, unpleasant consequences await.

This child remains in us all our lives. The child in us steps on the brake when we see a policemen, even though we are not speeding. The child in us wants to retaliate when we've been wronged, even though it may make no sense to do so.

When God created man and woman, He gave them but one warning: They were never to eat from the tree of the knowledge of good and evil, "for when you eat of it you will surely die" (Gen. 2:17). What a fateful warning! And when Adam and Eve did eat of the tree, they hid in the bushes from the face of God. That is what I mean by the fear of retribution!

When you consider the fact that in a denomination like mine (Southern Baptist Convention) the average age of persons at their baptism is nine, an interesting fact becomes apparent. Many of the persons in our churches made their entry into membership during this fear-of-retribution stage. I can remember well the night I first responded to an invitation to receive Christ as Savior. It was on Easter evening, and the visiting evangelist preached on hell. Out of a sense of dread—the fear of retribution—I responded. One thing I knew: I didn't want to go to hell! Since that time I have grown in my understanding of the gospel and in my commitment to Christ. I have other reasons for being a Christian now.

The Sinai Stage

As we follow biblical history, man indeed disobeyed God and faced the consequences of that rebellion: the loss of Eden. As lost humanity populated the earth, God began to reveal Himself to His fallen creatures. A method God has used to relate to us and to reveal Himself to us is covenant. A covenant is a contractual agreement between two parties. God made a covenant with Abraham, promising the man of faith a descendency of enormous population. In addition, Palestine was promised to Abraham and his heirs.

About four centuries after Abraham, Israel was anywhere but dwelling in the land of promise; the people were in bondage in Egypt. As God led His people out of Egypt under the leadership of Moses, He made yet another covenant with them at Sinai. The Mosaic covenant was different from the Abrahamic covenant in that it was conditional. The conditions were codified into law and summarized in the Ten Commandments. The people agreed to the terms. It was a corporate decision; they were all in it together.

By the time of Christ, the law of Moses was a topic of great interest. The underlying assumption was that it was very important to keep the law. But how to keep all these commandments in light of specific situations? Historical interpretations of the law had come to prominence. Rabbinical traditions and rules now outnumbered the original laws they sought to clarify. It was a confusing mess that only the Pharisees seemed to understand.

Jesus found great fault in the legal system of Judaism, especially the version fostered by the "experts." "You nullify the word of God for the sake of your tradition," Jesus said (Matt. 15:6). Though the law was a definite improvement over the days of every man doing what was right in his own eyes, it still broke down under its own weight. Why? How could rules be made to fit every conceivable situation?

What does it mean to not work on the sabbath? The folly of the legal absurdities is illustrated in such rules as not being able to put in your false teeth on the sabbath. (It was fine to wear them if you had them in before the sabbath came.) A wound could be attended to only so long as it was not made better. That would be healing on the sabbath, and healing was work.

A time comes in virtually everyone's life when he feels a need to systematize the contingencies that lead to punishment and reward. This leads to greater consistency in and control over environment. In addition, after the contingencies are delineated, they can be compared with the codes of others. When many people accept the same or similar set of codes, societal norms are established.

The systems, or rules, allow us to face daily situations with some degree of confidence. If Mama put me in the corner yesterday for drawing on the wall, I think I'll stick to the coloring book for today. In fact, I had better not draw on Grandma's walls either since she goes by the same rules as Mama.

Obviously conventions, or the recognition of systematized contingencies by large groups, are essential to the successful functioning of society. This is what we term *law and order* or *the rule of law*. Imagine what the world would be like without conventional thinking! One person would stop at a red light, another would go (not too far from reality, is it?). But what if a third of drivers drove on the right side, a third on the left, and the other third down the middle?

The operative word in the convention stage is *conformity*. Conventions are an advanced way of reciprocating. If you will stop at red lights, so will I, and likewise for the right side of the road. But who will be in charge of enforcing these conventions? That is where government comes in. The child is still in us, for we have conventionalized Mama and Daddy in government! The police officer will mete out retribution when we violate the codified conventions of society.

As an avid student of the law, Saul of Tarsus was one of its most zealous defenders. Eventually, however, the apostle Paul came to realize the inadequacies of the law:

For I would not have known what it was to covet if the law had not said, "Do not covet." But sin, seizing the opportunity afforded by the commandment, produced in me every kind of covetous desire. For apart from law, sin is dead. Once I was alive apart from law; but when the commandment came, sin sprang to life and I died. I found that the very commandment that was intended to bring life actually brought death (Rom. 7:7-10).

What is wrong with the law? Ask any police officer! The law cannot change people; it only points out their faults! As Paul continued his discussion of the law in Romans 7, he pointed out this fact: "I do not understand what I do. For what I want to do I do not do, but what I hate I do" (v. 15). The law was powerless to change Paul's "want to." And until our "want to's" are changed, we are doomed to continue breaking the law.

Finally, Paul concluded:

For what the law was powerless to do in that it was weakened by the sinful nature, God did by sending his own Son in the likeness of sinful man to be a sin offering. And so he condemned sin in sinful man, in order that the righteous requirements of the law might be fully met in us, who do not live according to the sinful nature but according to the Spirit (Rom. 8:3-4).

So we see there is yet another stage, a stage prophesied by Jeremiah long ago as the "new covenant":

"The time is coming," declares the Lord,
    "When I will make a new covenant
with the house of Israel
    and with the house of Judah.
It will not be like the covenant
    I made with their forefathers
when I took them by the hand
    to lead them out of Egypt,
because they broke my covenant,
    though I was a husband to them,"
            declares the Lord.
"This is the covenant I will make with the house of Israel
    after that time," declares the Lord.
"I will put my law in their minds
    and write it on their hearts.
I will be their God,
    and they will be my people" (Jer. 31:31-33).

The Calvary Stage

Centuries later, Jesus met with His disciples for the last time before His death and instituted the Lord's Supper. During that Passover meal, Jesus lifted the cup and said, "This is my blood of the new testament, which is shed for many for the remission of sins" (KJV). Following that meal, Jesus went forth to die on a Roman cross. By His resurrection, Jesus ushered in the new era of salvation by faith in Him.

Christ's work reveals to us the power that changes men and women. For as we each take up our own cross, we die to the old life and are born again into the life of Christ. Our desires, our attitudes, and even our actions are changed as a result.

> Therefore, I urge you, brothers, in view of God's mercy, to offer your bodies as living sacrifices, holy and pleasing to God—which is your spiritual worship. Do not conform any longer to the pattern of this world, but be transformed by the renewing of your mind. Then you will be able to test and approve what God's will is—his good, pleasing and perfect will (Rom. 12:1-2).

The operative word in the Calvary stage is *love*. Love is the only power that can change a person. Love fulfills the law. But, ultimately, love must break the law, for the law is only the conventions of human norms. If humanity is fallen, then the norms of human society must be fallen as well. Now, I'm not advocating an antinomian, radical departure from law and order. A good Christian is a good citizen. But there must come a departure from law to that which is higher.

Love is the highest form of reciprocity, for rather than saying, "I won't do this so you won't punish me" (Eden) or "I'll do this as you do also, for the better of us both" (Sinai), it says, "I'll do for you because God has done for me" (Calvary).

Many different things are said and done in the name of Christianity for a variety of reasons and from a variety of motivations. Some of what is done is from fear or trying to please a God who is perceived to be vindictive. Conventional values play a large role in the behavior of many (if not most) Christians. The fact that values are termed *conventional* indicates that society as a whole (or each subsociety in the church) functions at this level: on the basis of adopted standards. But for both of these stages, the reciprocity is basically negative, arising from a self-centered attitude.

A Calvary stage of reciprocity is unique in that it focuses upon the needs of others. Ministry from any other basis is ill-founded. True joy comes from selfless service.

The Fruit of the Spirit

Trying to attain joy is like trying to achieve strong muscles, good health, or even patience. All these ends are the results of processes. Therefore, this third ingredient in the joy formula is called *positive results.* Jesus said in John 15:8, "This is to my Father's glory, that you bear much fruit."

The fruit of the Spirit (Gal. 5:22-23) are the results of the indwelling Spirit's work in our lives. Through our relationship with Christ, we are "in Christ" and He is in us. In this vital union would grow a loving reciprocity. "Remain in me, and I will remain in you. No branch can bear fruit by itself; it must remain in the vine. Neither can you bear fruit unless you remain in me" (John 15:4).

Jesus had promised the coming Spirit, another Helper of the same kind as He, to indwell His followers (John 14:16-17). Out of this vital relationship and loving reciprocity would grow the fruit of the Christian life: the character of Christ and ministry.

Strong muscles are the result of consistent exercise. Health is the by-product of life-style. Patience is the harvest of endurance. Likewise joy cannot be attained as an end in and of itself; it is a result. The results are only clues to the effectiveness of the life process. If there are positive relationships centered in Christ and loving reciprocity, one of the results will be joy. The fact that there are many other wonderful results from this process only enhances the joy! In this way, joy is *responding* to the results positively.

Joy is not the same as happiness. Happiness arises when good things are happening. Joy may flow in abundance in the face of trying circumstances. Paul and Silas sang hymns of praise from a prison cell (Acts 16). Joseph summed up his brother's mistreatment with, "You intended to harm me, but God intended it for good" (Gen. 50:20). True joy enables us to release resentment, deal with insecurity, and cast off discontentment. "The joy of the Lord is your strength" (Neh. 4:10).

Notes

1. This is not to say that in cases of need the irresponsibility always lies with the needy. The plight of the homeless and hungry in our society is a symptom of irresponsible government and social systems as well. But this illustration is simply a case in point of the fact that for many "needy" persons, the greatest need is for some initiative and responsibility.

2. Bill Kellerman, "Apologist of Power: The Long Shadow of Reinhold Niebuhr's Christian Realism," *Sojourners,* Mar. 1987, p. 17.

3. Archibald Hunter, *The Gospel According to St. Paul* (Philadelphia: The Westminster Press, 1966), p. 34.

4. This discussion of stages is done at the risk of oversimplification. For readers interested in a more thorough treatment of moral-stage development theory, please consult the following: Dusk and Whelan, *Moral Development,* Paulist Press; Galbraith and Jones, *Moral Reasoning,* Greenhaven Press; Lande and Slade, *Stages: Understanding How You Make Your Moral Decisions,* Harper and Row; Susan Pagliuso, *Understanding Stages of Moral Development,* Paulist Press; Weeks and Evans, *Casebook for Christian Living,* John Knox; and Mary Wilcox, *Developmental Journey,* Abingdon.

1

When You're Tempted and Tumble

So, if you think you are standing firm, be careful that you don't fall! No temptation has seized you except what is common to man. And God is faithful; he will not let you be tempted beyond what you can bear. But when you are tempted, he will also provide a way out so that you can stand up under it (1 Cor. 10:12-13).

Leo Tolstoy, the great novelist and author of *War and Peace,* spent his early years in sinful living. The lure of sin overwhelmed him. He once wrote, "I knew where these voices came from. I knew they were destroying my happiness; I struggled, I lost. I fell asleep dreaming of fame and women . . . it was stronger than I."[1]

Maybe it wasn't fame or women that conquered you, but I'm sure you can relate to Tolstoy's plight. There has been a time when you were tempted, and you fell, or let us say, you *tumbled.* I used to have a theology professor who would talk about "falling and skinning your spiritual knees." To tumble is to skin more than your "spiritual knees"; it involves elbows, a broken nose, and perhaps a few bruised ribs.

When King David spied Bathsheba one night, he didn't experience a momentary lapse; he tumbled. "All the king's horses and all the king's men couldn't put" David together again.

Perhaps you could have helped it, but the desire was so strong, and the reasons so convincing at the time, that you went along with something you knew was wrong. As the apostle Paul said, "For what I do is not the good I want to do; no, the evil I do not want to do—this I keep on doing" (Rom. 7:19).

Perhaps sin has a toehold on your life. You can relate to the plight expressed by Paul: You feel powerless. Sin has usurped your freedom of choice. You are overwhelmed with guilt, but no matter how guilty you feel, you still can't shake it loose.

We can overcome. Temptation does not have to be a time of defeat for us, as it often is. The promise of God's Word is that God is able to deliver you from sin.

A Crucial Distinction

As we begin this discussion about temptation, we must establish one fact at the outset: *Temptation is not the same as sin.* Many people come away from temptation feeling guilty. "How could I even think such a thing?" they ask themselves. "That's horrible—I shouldn't even think such things!"

Have you ever tried not to think of a pink elephant? The more you try not to think of it the more you think of it! There is a difference between being tempted to sin and actually sinning. The Scripture says that Jesus was "tempted in every way, just as we are—yet was without sin" (Heb. 4:15). The Gospels record how Jesus was tempted in the wilderness, yet He didn't sin.

When Satan asked Jesus to turn the stones into bread, I'm sure Jesus thought how those round, smooth pieces of limestone resembled a loaf of bread! He was tempted, but He was sinless. Temptation and sin are not the same. Everybody is tempted. Even Jesus was tempted.

I believe great people have great temptations. The greater the person, the greater the position, the greater the power, the greater the ability, the greater the temptation. We easily condemn those in high offices who fall, but we don't always understand the nature of the temptations they face.

Let's look at what temptation really is. Temptation can be defined in at least three ways. First, the word *tempt* really means "to try" or "to test." This trial or testing can be positive or negative.

God tested Abraham. He told Abraham to sacrifice his only son. I once saw George C. Scott's portrayal of Abraham in the movie *The Bible.* I was stirred by Scott's rendition of what must have been a very trying experience for Abraham. But Abraham was faithful. God had to stop him—he passed the test.

But the testing can be negative too. When we are tempted to sin, that is negative. That does not come from God. James said that when we are tempted we should not say that God is tempting us because God is not tempted with evil and doesn't tempt us with evil. This negative side of temptation is of concern to us here. To tempt is to incite a person to sin.

Secondly, we could define temptation as *potential sin*. Temptation is any situation in which we could sin. It is some allurement to sin. The potential for sin is present, even though we may not sin.

I love to shoot guns. I have several guns of my own, and I like to go out to the firing range and shoot at targets. But I am afraid of guns. Guns have the potential for great destruction. I could kill someone with my gun. I could kill myself, if I'm not careful. To play with temptation is like playing with a loaded gun. The potential is there for negative consequences.

Temptation can be an allurement to fulfill good desires in the wrong way or to fulfill evil desires. Desires hold a vast potential in our lives: out of desire come intention and action.

Jesus had no evil desires, but He was tempted in the wilderness. Satan was trying to get Him to fulfill His good desires in a bad way. "Turn these stones into bread," Satan told Him. Jesus was hungry. What's wrong with being hungry? Nothing! It is a good desire. If we didn't get hungry we might not eat, and then we would die. God made us with this desire. But Jesus would not meet His needs in an inappropriate way. He saw something in the temptation of Satan that was evil. He wouldn't go along with it. He would not allow Satan to pull Him down to a lower level. "Man does not live on bread alone," Jesus replied, "but on every word that comes from the mouth of God" (Matt. 4:4).

We all have desires. There is nothing wrong with being hungry. Even sexual desires are God given. But there are sinful ways we can fulfill these desires.

A third way temptation could be defined is by saying that temptation *confronts us with a choice*. We have to decide. Temptation is not sin, but the outcome of our decisions may be sinful. How we respond to the temptation determines whether we have sinned. So every temptation gives us an opportunity to show our loyalty to God. Will we respond God's way, as Jesus did, or will we respond the human way? To paraphrase Shakespeare, "To sin or not to sin: that is the question"!

Every decision offers us the freedom to choose. Sinful decisions rob us of that freedom. Adam and Eve's sin was an exercise in their prerogative to choose, but it also deprived them of the blessed choices they could have made otherwise. Sinful living is a continual narrowing of our freedom until we finally are in bondage.

I know a young man who is a kleptomaniac—a thief. While living at home he worked various odd jobs, losing each one because of his habit. He has literally stolen from the blind. His life-style also attracted him to a rough crowd. One night he turned up at the hospital—with a bullet wound. He was ejected from a halfway house for stealing. He was beaten almost to death once when found stealing. Now he is on the street. His options are very few now. But he still has one option: repentance!

The Pathology of Desire

Sin is desire gone awry. It is an evil act or even just an evil intention. According to Jesus' teaching in the Sermon on the Mount, sin does not have to involve external action. It can involve the intention of the heart. Hatred is called murder. Lust is called adultery. This is where the line between temptation and sin is fuzzy for many people.

The rabbis used to close their eyes when they saw a woman so as not to lust after her. A "spiritual" man would have had a sore nose from running into things. I wonder what the old rabbis would do today, with the way people dress. Back then, women were completely covered up. How would they have dealt with a bikini or miniskirt?

An evil desire is a desire perverted. In Romans 1:26 Paul said, "God gave them over to shameful lusts." What is a shameful lust? According to Scripture, it is a strong desire that has a negative connotation. We should not set "our hearts on evil things" (1 Cor. 10:6).

In both Romans and 1 Corinthians, the example of sexual immorality is given. "Shameful lusts" in Romans refers to homosexuality. Many people today claim that homosexuality is simply a sexual orientation for certain people, and that it is just as normal for them as heterosexuality is for others. Paul referred to homosexuality as a "shameful lust," an evil, perverted desire. It is sinful to sexually desire a person of the same sex.

A pedophile is someone with a sexual lust for children. Such persons have perverted desires. It is a sexual desire that has become an unnatural and shameful passion. By consistently and regularly partaking of child pornography and expending their sexual energies while indulging in such lewd fantasies, a person bends or perverts desire into an unnatural channel of expression.

Gluttony is a perverted desire to eat. A glutton eats too much (don't many of us?). Covetousness is wanting what someone else has. You don't want one like it; you want *his*.

What about the desire to *not* eat? Anorexia nervosa is such a pathology. Persons will literally starve themselves to death while viewing themselves as overweight. This, too, is desire gone awry. Some would protest labeling such eating disorders as "sin." If such a label was meant in a judgmental way, I would agree. But the fact remains that it is a pathological desire—a "diseased" desire, a sickness.

Obviously, these special classes of pathology require more than moral fortitude to effect a cure. They require psychological and even medical treatment. We certainly should place no stigma on such illnesses, but we must be careful what we term an illness. Let the weight of personal responsibility rest where it belongs.

Let's take desire a step further: intention. Intention is an act on its way. It is when you plan or purpose to do something. Evil intentions are evil acts on the way. "But each one is tempted when, by his own evil desire, he is dragged away and enticed. Then, after desire has conceived, it gives birth to sin; and sin, when it is full-grown, gives birth to death" (Jas. 1:14-15).

Many young persons are concerned about sexual practices. Our society bombards them with sexual messages on television, radio, and movies; sexual temptation is positively portrayed in music, on billboards, everywhere. It is the number one item used to sell anything from cigarettes to cars to whiskey. The message is: Sex outside of marriage is OK; sex with anyone is OK.

People shouldn't play games with morality. Some would think, "Well, just as long as we don't actually have sex, it is OK." "We can make out and pet and go right up to the brink, but that's not as bad as actually doing it." What did Jesus say? He said that if a man looks at a woman to lust after her he commits adultery with her in his heart. Jesus is saying that an evil desire and an evil intention are sinful too—even if they have not yet become actions.

Perhaps a person hasn't decided if he or she can get away with sex outside of marriage. The person may wonder, *What if I get pregnant? Or get caught? Or if my parents find out?* He or she wants to and will, but hasn't found a way—yet. A person may want to smoke dope, but just hasn't been able to get it—yet. He may want to read porn, but hasn't bought it—yet. He may want to cheat on his income tax, but is afraid he'll get caught. He may feel like killing a certain person, but doesn't want to face the consequences. It is sin; temptation has already borne some of its fruit.

It Is a Battle You Can Win

Many great persons have taken great tumbles. One difference between great persons and others is not in their lack of mistakes, but in how they rebounded from them. David tumbled over Bathsheba, but rebounded in repentance. Peter collapsed in a heap of failure on the night of Jesus' betrayal, but later preached Christ boldly at Pentecost. John Mark blew it on a missionary journey, but was later considered "profitable" for the work (2 Tim. 4:10, KJV).

In order to understand how to overcome temptation, we must first understand *why we succumb to temptation.* Let's use what I call the "two-mule" illustration. For many years the Levi-Strauss company put a patch on the back of their blue jeans that pictured a man with two mules trying to tear a pair of Levis apart. The picture is to emphasize the strength of the garment.

Think of your real self as the garment. Pulling from either side are two strong mules. These represent the two incompatible forces that are at work in the life of every person: desire and conscience. As a missionary I once knew used to say, "The mule that gets fed the most is going to out-pull the other." The force we strengthen the most will be the prevailing force.

Let's take a specific example. A young man is dating an attractive young lady. Both are active members of a local church. The young woman dresses in such a way as to make herself most appealing to her boyfriend. The young man has begun to use after-shave and cologne advertised as "sexy and sensuous." Both of the young persons like to read popular magazines which contain suggestive portraits, advertisements, and stories. When they go out on dates, they often go to movies, many of which contain bed scenes. The actors model a philosophy of life that is not Christian. All in all, these two are "typical" youth.

Let's suppose that these two young people are involved in the church's youth group and have an interest in growing spiritually. Which force in their lives are they feeding the most? Would it be surprising to find them out "parking" after a date? Would it be shocking to later discover that they had been engaging in sexual intercourse? If they have fed the "mule" of desire, sooner or later that force will overpower whatever restraining forces their consciences can muster. The moral of the story is: Feed the right mule!

The tragedy of that illustration is its *reality*. Furthermore and sadly, the story seldom concludes at this point. What is a person's reaction to personal moral failure? The plot can develop in two directions. One, there will be great remorse and repentance. Two, and, more likely, there will be great remorse and a restructuring of the internal forces to repress the guilt rather than deal with it repentantly. The ensuing plot thickens into an ever more elaborate and disastrous result.

Too often, a moral failure such as has just been described will initiate a process with at least four definite stages. First, there will come the *rationalization* stage: "It's OK, we really do love each other." Or, "We got a little carried away last time." The real error of the action is explained away or denied. The situation is seen as "an exception to the rule." But guilt remains.

When moral failure is rationalized and the guilt remains, other behaviors must be invoked to subdue the moral anxiety. This *reaction* stage is a time when the young couple might become all the more active in the the church's youth ministry. They could possibly become two of the most committed and motivated of the youth—not to mention the most "spiritual." Yet the guilt feelings—and the immoral actions—continue.

Dogged by the persistent guilt and their inability to break with the immoral patterns—despite temporary reprieves—the couple lapses into a stage of *counterreaction*. The same guilt that motivated them to greater activity in "spiritual" things is now an intensified and overwhelming force. They revert to their rationalization with ever-greater allegiance and begin to exploit the sheer pleasure of their misbehavior. They have grown envious of immoral models who can engage freely in such behavior and enjoy it greatly. They find community and a sense of social belonging in the subculture that promotes such attitudes and behaviors. Soon the network of their relationships will include others who share these counterreaction values.

Finally, having narrowed their freedom with each step, the couple find themselves in the *addiction* stage. That which they once fought so hard to control is now in tyrannical control over them. The budding sexual impulses have now become a harvest of overpowering sexual desire. The mule has become a tiger.

In this type of situation, the sexual life-style may soon be absorbed into marriage, which "legitimizes" the action. However, sexual dysfunction or maladjustment may result from the latent guilt that remains.

Lest the story sound completely hopeless, I should point out that what maintained the immoral behavior was a steady diet for the desires which could not be overcome. Had the couple put their desires on a "crash diet" and begun to lavish their consciences and spiritual natures with plenteous food, things could have changed. This might have involved breaking off their relationship. It certainly would have required a great discipline to alter their life-styles. And this kind of discipline could have been initiated at any stage, even the last, though it would have grown increasingly harder.

These four stages are likely to occur with virtually any kind of immorality: alcohol and drug abuse, homosexuality and other sexual perversions, criminal behavior (such as theft), and even domestic violence.

During the American Revolution, a poorly organized, poorly supplied Continental Army effectively routed the superior military force of the British crown. What the Americans lacked in technology and supplies, they more than made up for in courage, motivation, and sacrifice.

In any war, the side that is willing to pay the greatest price is often the winner. Likewise, the war with temptation can be won. And, indeed, it is a war. It is an *intra*personal war; that is, it is *within* the person. Someone has said that human beings are "walking civil wars." How true this is! Strong forces within us are often, if not always, in tension with one another. It is a constant daily battle—one that can be won, but one that requires continual vigilance.

Bobby Leach was an Englishman who successfully went over Niagara Falls in a barrel, without serious injury. Later, Leach was walking down the street and slipped on an orange peel. The fall broke his leg!

"So, if you think you are standing firm, be careful that you don't fall!" the Bible says (1 Cor. 10:12). Sometimes it is relatively easy to withstand the onslaught of the temptation of "terrible" sins. You may not struggle with whether to murder someone, rape someone, rob a bank, or become a homosexual. But you may be tripped up on some seemingly insignificant thing.

We each struggle with our own unique temptation demons. What is a real struggle for me may not be for you. But you have your weaknesses. The tempter is no fool, for he will find your weakest point and give you the "double whammy." Peter warned: "Be self-controlled and alert. Your enemy the devil prowls around like a roaring lion looking for someone to devour" (1 Pet. 5:8).

Any successful campaign against temptation will involve a fourfold strategy.

1. Remember the Original Sin

Yes, I believe there is an original sin. It is *the sin*. It is the sin behind every sin. It is the first sin and the last sin. It is the most subtle of all sins. C. S. Lewis has put it well:

> There is one vice [from] which no man in the world is free; which every one in the world loathes when he sees it in someone else; and of which hardly any people, except Christians, ever imagine that they are guilty themselves. I have heard people admit that they are bad-tempered, or that they cannot keep their heads about girls or drink, or even that they are cowards. I do not think I have ever heard anyone who was not a Christian accuse himself of this vice.[2]

It is pride. Pride led Eve to eat the forbidden fruit. It was not greed, lust, or anger; it was her desire to be like God. That is pride, and that is the root of sin: to be like God—to usurp God's place—to deny God's authority.

Both James and Peter quoted Proverbs 3:34 when they spoke of overcoming sin. " 'God opposes the proud/but gives grace to the humble.' Submit yourselves, then, to God. Resist the devil, and he will flee from you," said James (4:6-7). Peter reiterated, "Humble yourselves, therefore, under God's mighty hand, that he may lift you up in due time" (1 Pet. 5:6).

The opposite of pride is humility. Humility involves the recognition of who we really are. We are not God; we are flesh and blood. We are "earthen vessels." We are apt to sin. An abiding awareness of this fundamental truth will help us maintain our guard.

2. Know that There Is a Way Out

"God is faithful; he will not let you be tempted beyond what you can bear. But when you are tempted, he will also provide a way out so that you can stand up under it" (1 Cor. 10:13). This is a precious promise from God. There is always a way out of temptation without sin.

While this promise encourages us to avail ourselves of the grace of God, it also indicts us when we seek to rationalize our sin. When we find within us the tendency to rationalize our intentions or justify our actions, we should ask ourselves two very candid questions. One, *Who shut you in?* Do you feel there is no way out, and the temptation is too powerful? Did God shut you in, or did you shut yourself in? Did the "devil make you do it"? Or did you allow yourself to become entrapped by remaining in tempting circumstances?

A person might even use this line of thinking as a rationalization: I've let myself get trapped, so I just as well go through with it. No! God's Word says, "He will provide a way out." The door of sin is not closed until you close it. There is always a way out, if you want it. The second question to ask is, *Do you really want out?*

Even a strong piece of metal will break if it is bent back and forth enough times. Under the constant pounding of the storm, eventually even the stoutest tree will uproot. So it is with temptation. Flee from it as Joseph fled from Potiphar's wife!

3. Submit to God

Paul's advice about facing temptation in 1 Corinthians 10 is prefaced by a discussion of Israel in the Exodus experience. For God's people, there were many spiritual lapses during the journey. There even came a time when the people complained against God. Drawing an application, Paul concluded, "We should not test the Lord, . . . And do not grumble" (v. 9-10).

Ask God, but do not question Him. We may rightly query our Lord as to the reasons for our struggles, but to call the motives of God into question is another matter! The key words for facing temptation are, "humble yourselves."

Submitting to God also involves depending upon Him. Cry out to God. Jesus, our High Priest, is present with us to make intercession. He knows the nature of our struggles (Heb. 4).

4. Praise the Lord

This may sound so simplistic: praise the Lord. Praise is the heart of Christian worship. It is an art to be practiced regularly by God's people. The Bible teaches that Christ shall adorn us with "a garment of praise instead of a spirit of despair" (Isa. 61:3; see Luke 4:16-21).

Praise is crucial in the overcoming of temptation for at least three reasons. First, praise puts things in proper perspective. God is to be adored, for He sits on the throne of the universe. Praise focuses our thoughts and prayers on the sovereign God and away from our problems. By focusing upon God, we see our problems in a different light. As we get a glimpse of God's sovereignty and power, we become more confident in His power to deliver us from temptation.

Second, the devil cannot stand praise. James's admonition to "resist the devil and he will flee from you" must surely presuppose praise on the Christian's part. Praise must sound like fingernails on a chalkboard to the demonic creatures.

A third rationale for praise is that it ushers in the Lord's power. Praise has a way of aligning us with God and His purpose. A result of acknowledging the lordship of the indwelling Spirit is that His power is released. Paul's testimony was that "when I am weak, then I am strong" (2 Cor. 12:10).

Notes

1. Leo Tolstoy quoted by Hardy R. Denham, Jr., "Sermon Illustrations," *Proclaim,* Jan. 1983, p. 35.

2. C. S. Lewis, *Mere Christianity* (New York: Macmillan Publishing Co., Inc., 1977), pp. 108 *ff.*

2

When You Have to Make a Sacrifice

In his sermon "Handling Life's Second Bests," Harry Emerson Fosdick recounted the suffering sacrifices of Adoniram Judson. Frustrated and diverted from his original desire to go to India, Judson eventually went to Burma. The biography of the great missionary is filled with accounts of trying circumstances and setbacks, yet stands as a life of great victory. Fosdick concluded, "and when the consequence began to appear he could look upon his life in retrospect as though it had been planned of God." Then Fosdick made an eloquent point of application: "To live your life through—not argue it through; that never is sufficient—to *live* your life through into the conviction that there is an eternal Purpose with which a man can ally himself is one of the finest achievements of the human spirit."[1]

One aspect of the teachings of Jesus and the New Testament writers goes unheeded today by vast numbers of modern Christians. The kind of message many want to hear these days is the message of prosperity. "Tell me how to prosper, how to have blessings. Give me the secret of healing. Tell me how to overcome financial struggle and be successful. How can I salve my guilty conscience? How can I avoid pain?" These are the kinds of things many people want to hear today.

"Don't talk to me about lordship," they say. "Don't talk to me about pain or complex problems. Speak nothing of doubts or sin. Don't talk to me about materialistic values." What is desired is a Christianity that is molded and remolded to fit comfortably within the ideals of modern culture with its mores. A "great" Christian, according to this model, is one who can have the best of both worlds: health, wealth, and success and eternal life to boot.

Was Paul referring to modern Christianity when he wrote, "For the time will come when men will not put up with sound doctrine. Instead, to suit their own desires, they will gather around them a great number of teachers to say what their itching ears want to hear" (2 Tim. 4:3-4)? Or is Paul's maxim "godliness with contentment is great gain" (1 Tim. 6:3-10) no longer true?

The Bible is not a negative book. It is a positively realistic book. It gives us a realistic view of life from the positive perspective of God's love and power. People are not all bad, and they are not all good. The characters in the Bible were not always righteous. They were human. But the Bible always presupposes the power of God to make good come out of less than good.

To espouse only a "health, wealth, and success" theology is to deny the realities of life. To preach only fire and brimstone and judgment all the time is to misrepresent God. A proper balance of all that Scripture teaches must be maintained. That is why Paul charged Timothy to "preach the Word; be prepared in season and out of season" (2 Tim. 4:2). Paul also told the Ephesian elders, "I have not hesitated to proclaim to you the whole will of God" (Acts 20:27). True biblical teaching properly represents *all* of the Bible.

The Bible does tell us about the blessed life, the good life. The Christian life *is* the good life. It is the best life——*the* life. There is no greater fulfillment than that which is found in serving the Lord. His blessings are abundant. His provisions are more than ample.

But to preach the biblical message is to talk about life from the perspective of a positive realism: to taste the sweet with the sour, to take the weal with the woe; the storms with the calm; the mountains with the valleys. Faith enables us to taste the sour with hope because we also know what the sweet is like.

Needless to say, sacrifice is not a popular topic. It is not an oft-used subject for inspirational literature. However, sacrifice is an integral part of the Christian experience. Sacrifice is a dominant theme in the teachings of Christ. It was the keynote of early Christianity. In fact, the biblical term *witness* comes from the same Greek word from which we get our English word *martyr*. There was a time, and there are times, when being a witness of Christ was to pay the supreme and sacrificial price. Are we above it? In our high American standard of living and religious freedom are we exempt from sacrificial service? Is sacrifice something that God has reserved for just a select few in a remote region of the world at brief moments in history? Or is sacrifice a common denominator among all Christians?

Without a proper understanding of sacrifice, situations of sacrifice might be misconstrued as abnormal or out of place in the Christian life. Some see sacrifice as a symptom of faltering faith or even as a slap in the face by the Almighty.

What is sacrifice? What does it mean to sacrifice? Webster's dictionary defines sacrifice as a giving up of one thing for the sake of another. The word comes from the Latin "to make sacred." Think about that! Anything we sacrifice for God or to God becomes sacred.

Of course, the greatest definition of sacrifice is the cross. In the cross act, God made the single greatest sacrifice ever: the life of His dear Son for you and me—a giving up of one thing for the sake of another. God gave up His Son for you, His righteous life for your unrighteousness, His perfection for your imperfections, His death for your life.

To talk at all about Christianity without including sacrifice is like playing a football game without the ball! Sacrifice is an essential element of Christianity: God's sacrifice for us and our sacrificial living in response.

When You Wish You Didn't Have to

Have you ever had to do something that you really didn't want to do? There are always some things we would rather not do, perhaps some things that we struggle hard to avoid. But if we are going to have a better life, be true to our convictions, or really help someone out, we must do it.

In Luke 14:25-35 Jesus talked about the cost of being a disciple. Strange words, indeed! Can you imagine Jesus talking about hating your parents, and even yourself? Can you picture yourself carrying your own cross? What about when Jesus said, "Any of you who does not give up everything he has cannot be my disciple"? That's not exactly the modern idea of how to win friends and influence people, is it?

Lest you get the idea that Luke 14 is an isolated passage, consider Jesus' remarks to the rich young ruler in Matthew 19:16-28. Sell *everything* and give it to the poor?

Jesus taught that anyone wanting to follow Him must "deny himself and take up his cross" (Mark 8:34), "be the very last, and the servant of all" (Mark 9:35), and "The man who loves his life will lose it, while the man who hates his life in this world will keep it for eternal life" (John 12:25). Paul enumerated a very long list of sacrifices and sufferings on his part for the cause of Christ in 2 Corinthians 11:23-33.

Somehow, this does not seem to jive with the concepts I read and hear taught today under the guise of successful Christian living.

The issue I want to emphasize is that the principle of sacrificial service cuts against the grain of our natural, human values. The *minimax principle* of group dynamics states: "People will join groups that provide them with the maximum number of valued rewards while incurring the fewest number of possible costs."[2]

Christians striving for church growth cannot afford to overlook the minimax principle: People will join the church they feel offers the best program and the least amount of required sacrifice. We must be careful lest we sacrifice the principles of true Christianity to the voracious appetite for numerical success! Don't mistake my point! Christianity offers its rewards, but they are not always the kind people are looking for: immediate, tangible benefits.

Even sacrifice can become a subtle form of status for the Christian. Some feel Paul was dangerously close to crossing the line into boasting in 2 Corinthians 11. But any advancement in spiritual growth is not without its price. It is hard to respect a Christian leader who is not willing to live sacrificially.

I recently saw a program on public television about monkeys and the social aspects of their lives. In the program, a monkey went from the lowest rank in the group to the highest by banging two empty kerosene cans together. This action scared the other monkeys into subservience. This portrayed for me the way some persons strive for prominence. They use noise and fanfare, achieving nothing in life but status. "What good is it for a man to gain the whole world," Jesus asked, "and yet lose or forfeit his very soul?"

The Christian life calls for sacrifice, but are we willing? I can witness, but I'm too shy. I can give, but I don't have much. I can be present, but I won't be missed if I don't attend. I can love, but I'm afraid to be hurt. I can help, but I'm not sure I can do any good. I can pray, but does God hear me?

The gift of sacrifice becomes precious to the recipient. Herein may lie one of the greatest benefits of sacrifice: the joy brought through ministry to the needs of another. During David's ongoing battle with Saul, he became thirsty as he and his men subsisted in the wilderness. Some of David's most loyal soldiers risked their lives to take a jug of water to their thirsty leader. David poured out the water his valiant men fetched for him. It became a sacrifice of thanksgiving. He was

not willing to lose the opportunity to live sacrificially with his men—
thereby tightening the bonds of identity and loyalty.

When You Have to Settle for Less

Sometimes we settle for less when we shouldn't, less than the best
our lives and churches can be. A man once shared during a testimony
service how as a youth he felt the call of God on his life for a preaching
ministry, but a tragic accident forced him to opt for a lesser form of
service. The real tragedy of that man's life was the bitterness he
carried within him and his unwillingness to accept the challenges life
presented him.

In contrast, I often think of a young man with whom I graduated
from seminary. My classmate has cerebral palsy. The braces he must
wear enable him to walk, though in a most pains-taking way. He
cannot speak clearly, write, or climb stairs. In fact, he uses his nose
to press the buttons on the elevator! Yet he made it through college
and seminary! I often wondered, *What can he do? What service can
he possibly perform? He can hardly even talk!* But, if nothing else, he
is a minister of inspiration! This man was not willing to settle for less
but did great things with what he had to give!

Many who receive less than others give more. My brother was born
with an eye problem called dyslexia or "reversed vision." This made
it difficult for him to learn to read. Yet he, too, has finished college
and seminary and is serving as a pastor. I am thankful he did not settle
for less.

"The kingdom of heaven is like treasure hidden in a field. When a
man found it, he hid it again, and then in his joy went and sold all
he had and bought that field" (Matt. 13:44-46). Opportunities for
sacrifice are an investment in greater things.

In the Old Testament, Joseph faced many sacrifices due to his ill
treatment at the hands of his brothers. Yet his purpose in life was
fulfilled by doing his best where he was. "Now, do not be distressed
and do not be angry with yourselves for selling me here, because it
was to save lives that God sent me ahead of you" (Gen. 45:5). Therein
is the hidden treasure of sacrifice!

Perhaps you feel that unless you have a big house, two cars, and
a boat, you are not successful. Maybe you consider yourself ungifted
when it comes to having something to offer. "What can I do?" you
ask. "I can't teach like this person. I'm not as outgoing or pretty or

intelligent or witty or articulate or aggressive as that person. What can I do? I don't have much money or talent or many friends. My health is bad."

We can think of a thousand reasons why we cannot do something or why we cannot reach our potential in life. But the real reason may be that our lives are different from what we would like them to be. Make the best of it!

Alfred Adler was a psychoanalytic theorist around the turn of the century. Having broken with Freud over Freud's determinism, Adler went on to found Individual Psychology and to become a foundational influence in modern psychotherapy. One of the basic premises of Adler's theory was based on his own life's experiences. As a child Adler experienced feelings of inferiority. He found that these feelings of inferiority drove him to seek superiority in his field. Later in life, his conversion to Christianity enabled him to more fully develop his theory as a positive expression of man's ability to overcome.

Paul had his "thorn in the flesh"; Roosevelt, his polio; George W. Truett, his bouts with depression; Helen Keller, her deafness and blindness; and T. B. Maston, his mentally handicapped son. Yet all these persons found the hidden treasures in their sacrifices. Great persons are not great because they have no hindrances or drawbacks or barriers to overcome. They are great because of them!

John L. Dagg was a leading Southern Baptist in the nineteenth century. He had little formal education. He taught himself, with the aid of his parents, Greek, Hebrew, and Latin. He became a schoolteacher at age fifteen. From age sixteen to twenty, he studied medicine until he fought in the War of 1812.

A jump from a window of a collapsing, burning building where he was preaching left Dagg lame at the age of twenty-nine. That same year he lost his wife in childbirth and his eyesight. At age forty he lost his voice and could thereafter speak only in a whisper.

In spite of his handicaps, Dagg achieved prominence as a leader. After the War of 1812, he became principal at Upperville Academy, where he lost his eyesight while studying Greek in the early mornings by the light of pine knots or candles. Wearing bandages over his eyes most of the time, he said, "Lame and blind, how could I be useful, and how provide for the wants of my children?"

Lame and blind, he was called to pastor Fifth Baptist Church in Philadelphia at age thirty-one, where he helped to found the Pennsylvania Baptist Convention. After nine years of preaching, he lost his voice.

Dagg resigned his pastorate at age forty and became president of Haddington College near Philadelphia, where he also served as professor of theology. At age forty-eight, he began his eight-year term as president of the Alabama Female Athenaeum.

Receiving an appointment as president and professor of theology of Mercer University, Dagg served as president for ten years and as professor for twenty years. Having invented a writing board, he began an illustrious writing career at age sixty. He produced several theological works which became the standards of his day.[3]

Yes, sometimes we have to settle for less than we expected. We must take less than we want. Perhaps our abilities are less than we would desire. But how sweet the sacrifices of those who persevere in spite of their handicaps!

Notes

1. Harry Emerson Fosdick, *Riverside Sermons* (New York: Harper and Brothers, 1958), p. 58.

2. Donelson R. Forsyth, *An Introduction to Group Dynamics* (Monterey: Brooks/Cole Publishing Company, 1983), pp. 62-63.

3. L. Russ Bush and Tom J. Nettles, *Baptists and the Bible* (Chicago: Moody Press, 1980), pp. 157-170.

3

When You've Been Wronged

After giving the disciples the Model Prayer (Matt. 6:9-15), Jesus gave this disturbing teaching: "For if you forgive men when they sin against you, your heavenly Father will also forgive you. But if you do not forgive men their sins, your Father will not forgive your sins." In so doing, Jesus underscored one important aspect of the prayer: "Forgive us our debts,/as we also have forgiven our debtors" (v. 12).

The apostle Paul seemed to have understood Jesus' teaching on forgiveness very well, for he continued the emphasis in his ministry. "Be kind and compassionate to one another, forgiving each other, just as in Christ God forgave you" (Eph. 4:32). "Bear with each other and forgive whatever grievances you may have against one another. Forgive as the Lord forgave you" (Col. 3:13). Are we to understand these statements as a radically idealistic viewpoint or as the attitude God wants all believers to emulate?

How can you possibly forgive others when they wrong you? Sometimes the wrong is so hurtful that the lasting consequences are difficult to overcome. How can wrongs of this magnitude be forgiven?

I believe it is necessary for persons to come to a point of real forgiveness. It is necessary for personal joy and mental health. Furthermore, it is necessary for a genuine testimony of God's grace. Herein is a process that can lead anyone to truly forgive. It may not be instantaneous or easy, but it is possible.

This is no abstract or purely academic treatment of the topic of forgiveness for me. This material comes out of my own hurts and experiences. This is a message from one who has been wronged— severely denigrated—by the undeserved malice of others. The truths presented come out of my own struggle to forgive. I am here to say that it can be done—you can forgive.

I can remember a day when I read the words of Jesus in Matthew

6:15 and felt a wave of guilt and helplessness flood over me. "If you do not forgive men their sins, your Father will not forgive your sins." Those words of our Lord thundered through my mind and reverberated from the inner caverns of my heart and soul. *Mark Jones, if you do not forgive those who have wronged you, neither will your Father forgive your wrongs!*

I was shaken. "Lord, I try and try, but still I find that I hate these people who have wronged me." All I could confess before the Lord was that I could only *want* to forgive them, but I was totally incapable of doing so. I felt condemned.

My hurt had fermented into hatred. The hatred had soured into bitterness. I helplessly reflected upon Hebrews 12:14-15, "Follow peace with all men, and holiness, without which no man shall see the Lord: looking diligently lest any man fail of the grace of God; lest any root of bitterness springing up trouble you, and thereby many be defiled" (KJV).

My strength left me. Even the routine of daily living became an unbearably difficult chore. Life went from one diversion to another. I buried myself in my work. Consequently I found myself overwhelmed by life. My bitterness was a canker sore, an open wound, festering and infected, never healing—a cancer was eating away at my vitality.

Then came the physical ailments: an ulcer, infections, kidney problems, and headaches. Sometimes it seemed that every joint in my body was aching. I went to bed exhausted and woke up tired.

It was a long struggle. But now I am free. I am a free man, and I want to share with you my freedom. Even though I have yet to work through all of my own difficulties, I have a burning desire to share with you what God can do.

We sometimes oversimplify things in church. People want to hear the easy answers to simple questions. Indeed, people want easy answers to complex questions. Life is neither easy nor simple. To believe otherwise is to adopt a superficial religion, a put-on, a panacea, a fanciful fantasy faith.

As a former pastor, with two seminary degrees, who spends virtually every day involved in the Lord's work, I am here to tell you that it is not easy being a Christian. Christian service for me is not just an aside but a vocation, a way of life. I am no supersaint, but I think I know a little about the Christian life, and it is not easy!

I hate to disappoint you, but I have no quick fixes, no magical formulas, no secret insights among the insiders, no direct lines to God. I do not get first-class mail from heaven. I have no red phone hot line to God. I've met a lot of Christians, but none without the common struggles of life.

I've got some more news for you. It wasn't easy for Jesus, either.

It takes time for God to do His work of grace in our lives. I hope you're ready for His work to be done in you. Have you been wronged? Cheated? Abused? Dehumanized? Violated? Perhaps you're not even sure you were right, either. Have you struggled with it to the point of struggling with your struggles? Perhaps things are ready to fall into place for you. But, most likely, it is something you are going to have to work through just as I have and am.

Notions of Forgiveness

One reason many of us find it so hard to forgive is because we have some mistaken ideas about forgiveness. Let's examine some commonly held assumptions among Christians about dealing with wrongs done to us.

First is the notion that *we should not get upset.* You've been abused, victimized, or targeted for violence, but don't get upset about it! The idea behind this absurdity is that anger is a de facto sinful emotion, that you are wrong if you are angry.

We are afraid of anger, especially our own. But why don't we face the fact that we get angry just as we get hungry—it's unavoidable. It is the way we were designed. To tell someone who has been wronged not to get angry is like telling a victim of a car crash not to bleed.

"But Jesus got angry," you might say. What is the reply? "Yes, but that was *righteous indignation.*" What is righteous indignation? Of course, it was righteous indignation when Jesus threw the money-changers out of the Temple! Can't we be righteously indignant about the wrongs done to us? Whether you do it righteously or not, you are going to get indignant.

The next mistaken idea about forgiveness is called *"forgive and forget."* Where in the Bible does it say to forget? How can we forget? It is a physiological impossibility! One theory of learning is that every experience you have ever had is stored in your mind. It is as if a videotape is continually recording every word, thought, and feeling, twenty-four hours a day, every day of our lives. And that tape is available for instant replay.

Years ago a brain surgeon was operating under local anesthesia; in other words, the patient was awake during the surgery. To his great surprise, the surgeon found that as he probed the patient's brain with electrodes, the patient was able to vividly remember events of her childhood. Many experiences are forgotten, only to be remembered later. We cannot totally forget.

When I was in college, I actually called a person who had hurt me terribly to ask forgiveness for harboring resentment against that person! That's a rather interesting turn of events. I felt guilty for my anger and recollection of this person's ill treatment. It should have been the other person who was on the guilt trip, not me! Why did I feel guilty? Because I was thinking wrongly about forgiveness and was consequently expecting the impossible of myself—namely, to forgive and forget. I couldn't forget it and blamed myself for not being able to forgive in a superhuman way. Guilt robs us of the ability to forgive.

A third belief about forgiveness is that *sin is only against God.* A friend once committed an overtly sinful act that hurt me deeply. I felt betrayed and humiliated. My friend felt terrible about it as well. In dealing with the guilt, my friend confessed to me that it was a sin against God and that he had asked God's forgiveness. Quoting from Psalm 51:4 (David's lament over his sin with Bathsheba) my friend said, "The Bible says, 'Against you, you only, have I sinned,' and I've asked God to forgive me." Great! The only problem is that my friend *never asked my forgiveness.*

In at least two passages, Jesus made it plain that we can sin against others. In Matthew 18:15 Jesus said, "If your brother *sins against you* . . ." (emphasis mine). Also, in Luke's version of the Lord's Prayer, Jesus said, "Forgive us our sins,/for we also forgive everyone who *sins against us*" (emphasis mine).

How can we resolve these Scriptures? Sin against another person is in fact a sin against God. First John 4:20 makes this clear: "If anyone says, 'I love God,' yet hates his brother, he is a liar. For anyone who does not love his brother, whom he has seen, cannot love God, whom he has not seen." Sin is both vertical (between man and God) and horizontal (between man and man). This makes clearer Paul's statement in Ephesians 2:16 about the atoning work of Christ on the cross effecting reconciliation between God and man and between man and man: "in this one body to reconcile both of them to God through the cross, by which he put to death their hostility."

My friend had set me up for a guilt trip, a one-way ticket to self-condemnation. Through the employment of faulty notions of forgiveness, I was converted from the innocent victim to a guilty participant, unable to forgive either my friend or myself.

A fourth misconception about forgiveness is that *we should avoid confrontation.* This is not only poor mental hygiene but also unbiblical. In Matthew 18, which is about the brother who sins against you, Jesus went on to say, "Go and show him his fault, just between the two of you" (v. 15). That sounds very close to confrontation to me! Confrontation does not have to involve a heated argument; it does involve a sincere, face-to-face expression of feeling.

Many Christians have the belief that it is wrong to express feelings so directly, that it is better to absorb the anger or pain and go on with a fake smile. To some, this the way Christ would have done it. Not so! Jesus could be very confrontive at times, such as when He snapped at Peter, "Get behind me, Satan!" In fact, sincere confrontation is necessary for positive growth and the development of authentic relationships. Many of the feelings of resentment people carry around in them could have been dealt with effectively through a direct confrontational approach. Had they come out with their feelings when the time was right, much suffering later could have been avoided.

Forgiveness Is Not a Feeling

What can we do to truly forgive? Before sharing a threefold process of forgiveness with you, let me emphasize one important reality about forgiveness. Forgiveness is not a feeling (or the absence of it); it is an *act.* Forgiveness is not a thought or an emotion; it is something you do (or don't do). This is borne out in the meaning of the biblical words for forgive.

In the Hebrew, there are three basic words for "forgive": *kaphar,* to cover; *nasa,* to lift up or away; and *salach,* to send away, let go. In the New Testament Greek, there are also three basic words translated "forgive": *apoluo,* to loose away; *charizomai,* to be gracious to; and *aphiemi,* to send or let off or away. In both languages, the most common word used has the connotation of sending away or letting go. These are all action words, not feeling words. While great emotion may accompany forgiveness, nevertheless forgiveness is an act.

Steps to Forgiveness

How can we let go of a wrong done to us? How can we send away the resentment and bitterness? Here are three things you must do to forgive. At least these three steps will send you well on your way to the forgiving act.

Recognize the Wrong

Recognize it for what it is: it is wrong. You have had an injustice perpetrated against you. You have been attacked, scandalized, denigrated. You have been wronged. Someone has sinned against you.

Establish the full objectivity of the wrong. Work with it until you see clearly what was your part and what was the other person's part. When you see your part, make it right. But do not get caught up in the guilt trap of blaming yourself for the whole thing. One brick doesn't build a house! If someone wronged you, it was wrong—his wrong. It was his fault. Maybe it was 5 percent your fault, but that makes it 95 percent his fault! Apologize and make restitution for your 5 percent, if necessary, but recognize his 95 percent!

Continue examining what happened until you can reduce it to an indisputable debt. If you are going to forgive your debtor, you first need to know how much he owes you!

One of two things may happen at this point. You will be tempted to think that the wrong is not significant enough, or you will think that it is too big to forgive. What if it looks insignificant? After you really look at the wrong, you say to yourself, "Oh, it was not that big a deal." Then why are you even considering it? If it is so minute and unimportant, why haven't you forgotten it altogether? You forget other meaningless, insignificant trivia; why not this issue? Maybe it is not so insignificant after all. Deal with it.

On the other hand, what about this impossible debt? The pain is just too great, the scars too noticeable. You've been left crippled by the experience. It is bigger than you and your power to forgive. Perhaps you try and try, but just cannot forgive. Or you may have no desire to forgive. You hate the person who wronged you so much that you hope some terrible catastrophe happens to him. You want revenge.

The Count of Monte Cristo was a character consumed with bitterness. He had been unjustly condemned to prison for life. His father died of hunger because there was no one to care for him. His beautiful girl erroneously heard that he had died and married another. One day the count escaped and eventually found a buried treasure. He purposed to use his wealth to get revenge. He did—perfect revenge. Not a stone of recompense was left unturned. But in the end he was left hollow and empty. Revenge had not satisfied him.

"Do not take revenge, my friends, but leave room for God's wrath, for it is written: 'It is mine to avenge; I will repay,' says the Lord" (Rom. 12:19). Do not usurp God's place. Let God be God. Just recognize the person's wrong for what it is. He sinned against you. Until you establish this crucial fact, you will not be able to deal honestly with the wrong done against you. You will lapse into bitterness or self-blame.

Recount the Wrong

This may sound like strange advice, particularly after what has just been said about not harboring desires of revenge. But if you neglect this very important step, you may fail altogether in arriving at true forgiveness.

Now let's suppose that you have reduced the wrong down to an indisputable debt. Then treat the debt as you would any other debt. Most of us know what it means to owe debts. We owe the bank for our cars, our houses, and all kinds of loans. But how does it feel to have someone owe you money? It feels good!

If you knew that someone owed you, and that the debt would eventually absolutely have to be repaid, you could live with that, couldn't you? Does not God promise that all these debts will be repaid? "I will repay," says the Lord.

That sin against you amounts to a debt with the cosignature of God Himself on the promissory note! It will be repaid; there will be justice. That is assured on the basis of the sure Word of God.

In Revelation, the cries of the martyrs are heard in chapter 6, "How long, Sovereign Lord, holy and true, until you judge the inhabitants of the earth and avenge our blood?" (v. 9-10). Following this, the trumpet judgments are sounded in direct response to this prayer!

You have been wronged. The God of justice will see that all wrongs are eventually made right. You will be vindicated. That debt is your asset; it is at your disposal. Recount it; assign to it a simple definable value. What is it worth to you?

Sit down and make out a ledger sheet. Accounts Receivable: debts owed to you. You have a judgment against these wrongdoers in the court of heaven. There is no escape. No chapter eleven bankruptcy. It will be paid. Write down the debt: name, sin, and amount. Was it your reputation? Write, "Owes me my reputation, my good name." The debt is public restitution of your good name. The debt could be money, health, happiness, or the life of a loved one.

Total what your debtor owes. Maybe it is a massive amount. How much would it all be in dollars? Beyond monetary equivalence? How much would it be in years or in joy? What are the debts worth?

You are rich! And with riches you have power! You are the debtee! Those debts are in your hand! Jesus told Peter that whatever he loosed on earth would be loosed in heaven; whatever he bound on earth would be bound in heaven. You have the power of those debts in your hand. Enjoy it!

Recount those debts. Hold them close to you. Carry them with you wherever you go. Keep the list in your pocket. Pull out the list often and read it. Total the figures again! This time include interest! Don't forget to factor in inflation!

Carry those debts until they become an albatross around your neck. Carry them until they become a weary burden. Tie them to you until they become so much baggage. Stay up nights to count them and total them until your eyes are bloodshot.

Now you've become like the man who all his life wanted riches. He poured his life into attaining wealth. With the riches came responsibility. He had businesses to administer, bills to pay, taxes to figure, spoiled kids to rear, a wife to please, new enemies, and new friends who wanted only his money. Soon he longed for the simple days of his poverty.

Release the Wrong

Now comes your opportunity to wield that new power you have! It is your prerogative; exercise it! The ball is in your court now! It is in your hand! It is your authority, your initiative, your account, your right.

Total those debts. Make only one copy: The only proof of all these debts must be in one single envelope. Seal it.

Now write across that envelope, "Paid in full. All debts released." Date it. Sign it. Burn it. Watch it go up in smoke, all those debts . . . turned to ashes. Now you're free.

When Jesus hung on the cross He cried out, "It is finished!" God had fulfilled His promise, and He had paid the full price for our forgiveness. Because of the gracious and free forgiveness of Christ, can you now forgive your debtors?

4

When It's Hard to Believe Anymore

For some of my classmates, college was a time of doubting. If the biology and psychology classes didn't jar your faith, the philosophy professor considered shaking up students one of his specialties. For me college was an intense and thought-stimulating time of grappling with many issues. But by God's grace, I graduated with faith intact. I had made it, I felt, and was ready to plow right into graduate theology studies at seminary. Somewhere between my first and second seminary degrees doubt struck me—like a mugger waiting in the shadows—catching me off guard.

The "mugger" was a theologian who had authored one of the texts used in a doctoral seminar on church renewal. That man punched, jabbed, and lampooned my faith until I swooned like a glazed boxer. I was down for the count and carried from the ring. I didn't even hear the bell.

Looking back from the perspective of a wisdom that knows better than to ever again set foot in the ring with a heavyweight, I can see that I was preoccupied. Many stresses had distracted me from my conditioning. It was a set-up. I was doomed by my own naïveté to take a fall. I was tall and skinny in my spiritual life, which made the crashing timber hit with all the more resolve. Doesn't the ground feel hard when you land face down?

There were days when it was victory just to muster enough plastic faith to get me through Sunday morning sermons. Afterward I would hobble, gasping, back into my study to catch my breath in the seclusion of my private pilgrimage. I was like the tail-chasing dog who yelped every time he took a bite, never realizing the connection. My theological doubts were coming from somewhere. That author didn't do it to me all by himself; I was framed. I had yet to ask myself what I was doing in that part of town to start with.

How many times I had sat in my study, or stood by a hospital bed, and listened to some poor soul pour out his or her discontent with God. I had been called upon countless times to perform emergency surgery on these persons' faith. It was clear as daylight to me, as I diagnosed each case, that crises had precipitated a glitch of faith. Take two psalms and call me in the morning. After all, nobody finds lost faith overnight. We'll work on it tomorrow. Just rest easy. Maybe a sedating prayer or two to calm the nerves.

Why couldn't I see what was happening in my own life? My faith had trickled down a winding Jordan until it had just about stagnated in the Dead Sea of weariness. I talked God and sang God, but inside I felt that He had slipped offstage and left me to dance alone. Finally my thought became, "What's the use?"

Have you ever thought you had found paradise, only to discover it was an island inhabited by cannibals? The youngest son of Jesse may have felt such confusion. Samuel annointed David king when there was already a king. Saul was showing signs of paranoia and David would soon be wondering about his own sanity.

David went from hero to hunted and had a real problem telling the good guys from the bad guys because the good guys *were* the bad guys. Even the bad guys (Philistines) became the good guys to David. It is likely that during this time in David's life Psalm 22 was composed. Things were going crazy for David, and he clung to his faith. Just remember, this psalm was on Jesus' mind when He clung to His cross. Maybe there is something in that psalm for you too.

It's Hard to Believe When Trouble Comes

Let's start with the obvious. For a man brought up in a religion that taught blessings for goodness, David was bewildered. The better he got at being good, the more flak he caught. Something had gone wrong with the universe.

C. S. Lewis spent a career interpreting the Christian faith. Many must have thought he had a direct avenue to spiritual reality. But when Lewis's wife died of cancer, the door of the sense of God's presence shut. Grief honors no exemptions. A thorough and working knowledge of Christianity does not preclude one from pain and its consequences upon faith. Lewis described his spiritual emptiness in approaching God as a door slamming "in your face, and a sound of bolting and double bolting on the inside. After that, silence. You may as well turn away."[1] It is hard to believe anymore when trouble slams the door.

David thought he heard a triple bolting of faith's door. His troubles were threefold. First, there was the pain.

> My God, my God, why have you forsaken me?
>> Why are you so far from saving me,
>> so far from the words of my groaning?
> O my God, I cry out day by day, but you do not answer,
>> by night, and am not silent (vv. 1-2).

David groaned and cried for God's deliverance. Some scholars believe the experience David is referring to was that described in 1 Samuel 23:25 *ff.*, when Saul and his armies were in hot pursuit of David. In fact, the two groups were so close that they could see each other across a valley. David was spared in the nick of time when an emergency message detoured Saul from the chase.

In such a situation, David would have suffered much from the anxiety, stress, and discomforts of a fugitive's life, with the added burden of knowing he was hated without cause. Anyone who has been falsely accused and publicly slandered can identify with David's expression of pain. Shakespeare said it well in *Othello:*

> Good name in man and woman, dear my lord,
> Is the immediate jewel of their souls:
> Who steals my purse steals trash; 'tis something, nothing;
> 'Twas mine, 'tis his, and has been slave to thousands;
> But he that filches from me my good name
> Robs me of that which not enriches him,
> And makes me poor indeed (III, iii, 155).

Gossip and rumors were rampant in the church. Some of the members had taken up a vendetta against the pastor. In a business session a man stood and angrily denounced the minister; the pastor's wife could stand no more of the sham. Marching up the center aisle of the session, she pointed her finger in the slanderer's face and sternly warned for all to hear, "If you do not quit telling lies about my husband, I'll start telling the truth about you!"

Who knows what hurt and injury lie hidden by the calm exteriors of church members? Christians in the pew and pulpit alike are susceptible to the corroding effect of pain upon their faith. Of course, I am using pain as a general term, for pain can encompass physical, psychological, and spiritual realms. Grief is the pain of loss. Anger is the pain of frustration. Doubt is the pain of a faltering faith. Who is to say which hurts more, a broken leg or a broken heart? David's anxiety took on huge proportions.

> I am poured out like water,
>   and all my bones are out of joint.
> My heart has turned to wax;
>   it has melted away within me.
> My strength is dried up like a potsherd,
>   and my tongue sticks to the roof of my mouth;
>   you lay me in the dust of death.
> Dogs have surrounded me;
>   a band of evil men has encircled me,
>   they have pierced my hands and feet.
> I can count all my bones;
>   people stare and gloat over me (vv. 14-17).

It is not surprising that our Lord could identify with this psalm during His passion!

Have you ever felt this way? Has stress, fear, or anger taken their toll on your physical health until you felt like a wreck? Should we not think that such denigration will tax our spirits as well? When evil staggers into our lives like an inebriated bull in a china closet, should we not wonder why? It is difficult to believe and hurt at the same time.

Studies have shown that people tend to interpret their pain by one of three spiritual categories: as punishment, as opportunity for transcendence, or as redemptive.[2] After an excruciating illness and postoperative recovery, a hospital patient once told me with a laugh, "I've paid for every sin I ever committed." He was enduing his pain with a punitive meaning. Suffering, for him, was the antecedent of sin.

Pain as a redemptive, salvific activity is a meaning given to suffering whereby one is effecting salvation on the part of self or others. This is a fairly common interpretation given to pain by sufferers, but one which, in my opinion, belongs exclusively to Christ. Paul, however, came close to this interpretation in Colossians 1:24: "Now I rejoice in what was suffered for you, and I fill up in my flesh what is still lacking in regard to Christ's afflictions, for the sake of his body, which is the church." The sufferer who calmly endures pain with dignity for the benefit that may be bestowed upon someone else is a likely example.

David's interpretation of his pain probably falls into the transcendence category. Like Job, David felt he was suffering unjustly, as an innocent victim. "Why me, Lord?" is the question of one who seeks to rise above the confusion brought on by seemingly meaningless pain. David was disillusioned with God's apparent inactivity to rescue him. "Why have you forsaken me?/Why are you so far from saving me?" (v. 1). As Job was able to transcend his suffering by humbly submitting to God's mysterious and all-wise plan, David confessed that God is "enthroned as the Holy One; . . . the praise of Israel" (v. 3).

On the subject of suffering, in Romans 8, Paul linked pain with eschatological hope when he considered "that our present sufferings are not worth comparing with the glory that will be revealed in us" (v. 18) and that "we know that in all things God works for the good of those who love him" (v. 28). In fact, Paul had learned to "delight in weaknesses, in insults, in hardships, in persecutions, in difficulties. For when I am weak," he said, "then I am strong" (2 Cor. 12:10). Paul rose above his pain by trusting in some higher divine, though unknown, purpose, thus preserving his faith.

When the element of malicious intent on the part of others is introduced, the problem of pain and faith becomes all the more complicated. David's pain was compounded by others' malice in two ways. First, they mocked his faith.

> But I am a worm and not a man,
>   scorned by men and despised by the people.
> All who see me mock me;
>   they hurl insults, shaking their heads:
> "He trusts in the LORD;
>   let the LORD rescue him.
> Let him deliver him,
>   since he delights in him" (vv. 6-8).

As if it were not bad enough for David's enemies to "filch his good name," they were after his religion as well. Indictments against our faith can be subtle. To ridicule one's faith is a serious insult, for it calls into question not only the reality of God's existence and love but our own worth as well. To mock a person's religion is to desecrate all that he is and stands for. This may be the essence of the derision of Job's wife when she said to him, "Are you still holding on to your integrity? Curse God and die!" (Job 2:9). Mocking a person's faith ought to be considered a violation of one's constitutional right of freedom of religion!

A second complicating factor of David's pain was the mistreatment he received (unless you think ducking spears is good fun).

> Many bulls surround me;
>> strong bulls of Bashan encircle me.
> Roaring lions tearing their prey
>> open their mouths wide against me.
> They divide my garments among them
>> and cast lots for my clothing (vv. 12-13,18).

David felt his situation to be hopeless, aside from the Lord's intervention. His abuse was physical and emotional as he fled through the desert regions to escape his insidious foe. The spiritual abuse came in the form of the mockings of his faith.

Child abuse is a problem of terrible proportions in our society. I have known persons who carry the emotional scars of child abuse. I cringe at the thought of others who are enduring an abusive relationship with their spouse. They feel despair, fear, and anger. Perhaps you know personally about this painful reality. This psalm of David is the cry of one who is experiencing untold abuse and heartache. Does it echo your sentiments?

It's Hard to Believe Until We Remember the Past

"O God, our help in ages past,/Our hope for years to come" begins one of my favorite hymns. We cannot know what the "years to come" will hold, but we can know that the "God of ages past" holds them! Even though David was exploring the depths of despair and agony, he was able to breathe a sigh of hope because of his experience of God's faithfulness in the past. Actually, it is a rather simple proposition: As God has been, He surely will be.

> In you our fathers put their trust;
>> they trusted and you delivered them.
> They cried to you and were saved;
>> in you they trusted and were not disappointed.
> Yet you brought me out of the womb;
>> you made me trust in you
>> even at my mother's breast.
> From birth I was cast upon you;

from my mother's womb you have been my God.
  Do not be far from me,
    for trouble is near
    and there is no one to help (4-5,9-11).

Erik Erikson postulates a model of psychological development which theorizes that persons go through a series of predictable crises as they grow throughout life. Sound emotional growth, for Erikson, involves successfully coping with each of these developmental crises. Interestingly enough, Erikson states that life's first crisis is trust versus mistrust. As a child enters the world, the capacity for basic trust can be developed only as the child experiences a world which consistently meets her or his needs. This reverberates in the statement of verses 9-10.

When taken in light of the mocking insult of verse 8, "He trusts in the Lord," David's reflection on God's faithfulness is significant. David had learned basic trust because of God's sure provision in the past, even as a baby has learned to trust his mother to feed him. Therefore, it was inconceivable for David that God would forsake him then.

Quite honestly, there are times in life when I would find it impossible to keep the faith were it not for previous experiences which taught me about God's goodness. Those experiences see me through the confusing times when it seems that God's hand has turned against me.

God gives the capacity to believe. "You made me trust in you," David said. This fact is resounded in Ephesians 2:8: "For it is by grace you have been saved, through faith—and this not from yourselves, *it is the gift of God*" (emphasis mine).

Call Out to God When It's Hard to Believe

I know a man who was lying in his bunk on ship when the Japanese attacked Pearl Harbor. His ship was badly damaged. At first, he could only guess what had happened. There were thundering explosions followed by pitch darkness. The sailors found themselves trapped below deck. Unable to see and standing in chest-deep water, this sailor tied his arm to his bunk with an electrical cord and waited in hope for more than twenty hours before being rescued. "We all knew they'd get us out," he once told me. Those hours must have seemed like days!

His arm is still partially paralyzed from the extended period of being moored to his bunk: a perpetual reminder of that ghastly experience!

In the psalm, David "turns the corner" in verse 19, "But you, O LORD, be not far off;/O my Strength, come quickly to help me." By calling out to God, David was taking a crucial step of faith. As the writer of Hebrews explained, "Anyone who comes to him must believe that he exists and that he rewards those who earnestly seek him" (11:6). Faith is claiming that which cannot be seen. Sometimes the darkness of trials obscures the face of God. David was reaching out to God from the darkness of his soul, to grasp the invisible reality of God's presence. "Deliver my life from the sword,/. . . . /Rescue me from the mouth of the lions;/save me" (vv. 20-21).

Faith breeds faith. Even the most minute expression of faith can be cultivated and nurtured into a mighty, life-altering force. At first, faith may be little more than a thought of God. But that one thought can serve as a piton on the sheer walls of trouble, from which a sure hold can be secured.

Since God exists, we can call upon Him. Since we can call upon Him, surely He will listen. Since He will listen, surely He will help. Scripture provides ample proof. For example, "This poor man called, and the LORD heard him;/he saved him out of all his troubles" (Ps. 34:6), and "This is the assurance we have in approaching God: that if we ask anything according to his will, he hears us. And if we know that he hears us—whatever we ask—we know that we have what we asked of him" (1 John 5:14-15).

God Is at Work Even When It's Hard to Believe

One of the sweetest aspects of Christian fellowship occurs when believers share their experiences of God's deliverance and provision. When I am wrestling with a problem, I am encouraged when I hear others recount how God saw them through similar situations. This may well be the idea behind the votive offerings of the Old Testament. Votive offerings were sacrifices brought to the Temple in fulfillment of a vow, perhaps made during a crisis. As the worshiper fulfilled his sacrificial vow, he gave a testimony of God's faithfulness.

Psalm 22 is probably a votive psalm, written by one who would not forget to give thanks to the God who delivers.

I will declare your name to my brothers;

in the congregation I will praise you.
From you comes my praise in the great assembly;
before those who fear you will I fulfill my vows (vv. 22,25).

David's faith transformed past truth into present reality and future hope. Verse 31, "They will proclaim his righteousness/to a people yet unborn," is another way of saying, "He did it for me; he'll do it for you!" In this way, David described the nature of God. Our Lord is the God of deliverance. It is His nature and desire to deliver. The psalm's conclusion points to the ultimate, eschatological deliverance of God. His people have borne testimony throughout the ages of His deliverance. "Posterity will serve him;/future generations will be told about the Lord" (v. 30). As He has been and is, so He surely shall be!

Notes

1. C. S. Lewis, *A Grief Observed* (Greenwich: Seabury Press, 1963), p. 9.
2. William L. Conwill, "Chronic Pain Conceptualization and Religious Interpretation," *Journal of Religion and Health,* 25, No. 1 (Spring 1986), pp. 46-50.

5

When You Don't Follow Through

During the Civil War in our country, on one particular night the troops were gathered around the campfires. The next morning they were to go into battle. As they sat around the fires that evening, with anxiety running high, one trooper was sharing stories about his own valor and prowess on the battlefield. He was telling his fellow soldiers about how he had been brave in the face of the onslaught.

Over the campfires, the soldiers were baking loaves of corn bread. The braggart placed one of the loaves in his coat pocket so he would have something to eat the next day, when there would be little time to prepare a meal.

The next morning the battle came and the men marched off into war. At the first sound of artillery, this "brave" man turned and ran like a scared chicken. He ran through and across fields. He ran as fast as he could. Then he came to a tall wall. Scurrying over the wall, he leaped from the top unaware that his corn bread had come out of his pocket. As he landed on the ground, the corn bread fell on top of his head. Feeling the thump, he jumped to his feet with his hands in the air saying, "I surrender, Sir!" He was the only person ever taken captive by his own corn bread!

It is easy to make commitments and boast of our courage and fortitude. But when the heat of battle comes, we can find our courage and fortitude slipping away from us. John Mark may have been such a person. In Acts 15 Luke recorded a heated discussion which took place between Paul and his fellow missionary Barnabas over John Mark.

> Some time later Paul said to Barnabas, "Let us go back and visit the brothers in all the towns where we preached the word of the Lord and see how they are doing." Barnabas wanted to take John, also called

Mark, with them, but Paul did not think it wise to take him, because he had deserted them in Pamphylia and had not continued with them in the work. They had such a sharp disagreement that they parted company. Barnabas took Mark and sailed for Cyprus, but Paul chose Silas and left, commended by the brothers to the grace of the Lord (Acts 15:36-40).

What is the background of this young man, John Mark? We first encounter him on the pages of Scripture in Acts 12. In this situation, Peter had been thrown in prison by Herod. The future did not look good for Peter. Herod had already put James to death. Finding that this pleased the Jews, he decided to do the same with Peter.

That evening, an angel rescued Peter from prison. Meanwhile, the disciples had gathered for an all-night prayer meeting for Peter's deliverance. Peter, brought to the street by the angel, realizing what had happened, went to the house where the disciples were praying and knocked on the door. It was the house where John Mark lived.

One can imagine the excitement as the disciples were praying and found that God had answered their prayers that very evening! In fact, when Peter first came to the door, they thought it was a ghost! It was difficult for them to believe in Peter's miraculous, sensational deliverance. What an impression that experience must have made upon young John Mark!

John Mark is referred to again in Acts 12:25: "When Barnabas and Saul had finished their mission, they returned from Jerusalem, taking with them John, also called Mark." John Mark had attached himself to these missionaries. On their first missionary journey, they took John Mark along. According to Acts 13:5, "John was with them as their helper."

The next thing one reads about John Mark is that he was going home. He had given up the journey and departed (v. 13). He left them in Pamphylia.

When Paul and Barnabas returned from that missionary journey and were discussing the prospects of taking another mission trip, Barnabas said that he wanted to take John Mark with them. Paul wouldn't hear of it. "Why take this young man with us?" we could surmise Paul to have said. "He's already left us once. He deserted us in Pamphylia. He couldn't make it the whole way. He quit. Why take him again?"

The argument was so heated that Paul and Barnabas parted ways.

I have often wondered who was right. Luke gave a hint at his opinion in Acts 15:39, "But Paul chose Silas and left, *commended by the brothers* to the grace of the Lord" (emphasis mine). The church put their blessings on Paul and his new partner Silas. Barnabas took John Mark and left for Cyprus. Scripture does not record the events or outcome of their mission.

At first glance it might appear that Paul was being rather harsh (and at second glance too). But Paul considered himself to be a soldier of the gospel. The Lord Jesus Christ came first in his life, and he was dead serious about the work of the kingdom. He would not have someone accompany him who could not stand up to the rigors of missionary work.

John Mark had not followed through with his commitment. Unfortunately, this is something virtually every Christian can identify with. We have all made commitments we did not keep.

There are many people like John Mark who sense the "call" of God on their lives to some missionary or ministry endeavor. It may be to go to another land or to a Sunday School class or to help in some effort. Emotion runs high, and commitment runs deep until the realities of service set in, testing loyalties.

A man came to his pastor's study and said, "I would like to be the director of the training program of our church." The pastor explained to him everything that would be involved. He would have to see that the records were maintained, promote the various opportunities, keep up with the classes, and organize teachers' meetings each week, among other things. "Yes, that is exactly what I want to do," was the response. So the pastor turned the job over to him. He spent that whole week at the church nagging the secretary and getting all the files in order.

Sunday came. No training director. The next week the office was back to normal with no training director shuffling through the files. That big flurry of inspiration and commitment vanished as quickly as it came. The pastor was left wondering how he could possibly build a solid church program on the basis of *that* kind of commitment.

Jesus said that anyone who puts the hand to the plow and looks back is not fit for the kingdom of heaven. The kingdom requires a commitment from all believers—not just an emotional jag, but a lifetime of commitment and service to our Lord.

Many people today, everyday, stand before an altar or judge and covenant with one another, declaring their love and loyalty to one another, entering into marriage. They promise that they will be faithful and true all of their lives to their marital partner. It is a contractual agreement, a vow. Yet almost half of every one of those marriages ends in divorce. It is as if people enter into the relationship with good intentions, sincerity of heart, pledging their love. Perhaps they are caught up in romantic love or infatuation. But then the tedium sets in. People may change. The marriage disintegrates over the years. Though they made a commitment, they later back out.

John Mark was not the only disciple of Christ who acted on impulse. Simon Peter shared this trait. Jesus said to Peter, "You are Peter, and on this rock I will build my church" (Matt. 16:18). Jesus was in essence redefining Peter's name. Peter means "rock." It was a play on words.

Surely from the beginning, Jesus saw something impulsive about Peter. He was a man who was quick to speak, slow to think. Peter was the type who would quickly jump into an issue or jump to conclusions or to make a commitment. Yet Jesus was able to take Peter, the "rolling stone," and make of him a foundation rock of service. The Peter we see after the resurrection of Christ, and after Pentecost, is a different kind of Peter. Christ had polished Peter's rough edges to produce a beautiful gem of a man.

God can see into our hearts and see the inconsistencies between what we say and what we do, between what we want and what we get. He can see the commitments that we have backed out of and the contradictions in our lives. But He can also see the potential if we will put our "hands to the plow" and keep our eyes forward.

As a teenager, I decided one day that I wanted to teach a Sunday School class. The pastor was delighted and assigned me to a class of older boys. It was exciting, and I spent hours preparing my lessons. But the boys were rowdy. They were more interested in discussing their favorite horror movies than in talking about the Bible. I stuck it out for several months, but I finally gave up in youthful impatience. The struggles of my own spiritual life and the demands of the class were just too much for me.

In my class was a young man who seemed to be much like the other boys. Most of them were from poor homes. Later I learned that this boy, in the sixth grade, was arrested for using drugs. I was shocked!

Then I was saddened as I realized that I possibly could have had some positive influence in that boy's life had I stayed with my commitment.

By pondering the results of failed commitments, we can learn the importance of following through. Let me give you three things to think about in regard to keeping commitments. How much more effective would be the work of our churches if we would keep these three ideas in mind as we serve Christ and each other.

Considering Our Fellow Christians

One result of not following through on commitments is that we let our fellow Christians down. That is what had happened to Paul and Barnabas. They had taken John Mark with them. They had made room for him, giving him a part of the work. And then he quit! Right in midstream he quit and went home.

In many ways it is understandable that Paul should react so strongly to Barnabas's idea of taking John Mark along the next time. Paul obviously felt that John Mark had not matured to the point that he could be an asset on the upcoming mission trip.

People have made investments in our lives. Fellow believers depend upon us. When we quit, do not follow through, walk away, or fail to show, we create a hardship for them. We let them down.

The typewriter was invented in 1868. It was a rather crude machine compared to the electronic models we have today. As the typewriter began to have wide distribution and people became proficient in using this new machine, a problem arose. There was a design flaw in the typewriter. The keys kept jamming. Those who could type fast were frustrated by this shortcoming. So the inventor redesigned the keyboard to alleviate the problem: The keys which were used most often were placed in the hardest-to-reach places using the weakest fingers! This had the effect of slowing down the typists and thus circumventing the problem of jamming.[1]

Some people have a problem inside of their lives. Rather than finding a solution to their problem, they want everyone else to accommodate them and to make up for their deficiencies.

The Christian life is a shared life. We are all in it together. One of the biblical metaphors of the church is that of a body. Some members are arms, some are legs, and others are various parts of the body. But each member is a part of the same body. If one part of the body is not functioning properly, all of the body suffers.

Peter used the metaphor of a house to describe the church. Each member is one of the stones making up the house. Can one imagine a house with part of the stones missing? In some ways, that is the way the house of God looks! Some stones are missing; some parts of the body are not functioning. As a result, the whole body is suffering. We support our fellow Christians by remaining true to our commitments.

Representing the Cause of Christ

A second result of not following through is that we put the cause of Christ in a bad light. By keeping commitments believers "show that they can be fully trusted, so that in every way they will make the teaching about God our Savior attractive" (Titus 2:10). The only Christ many people will ever see is the Christ that is in you.

How can we profess to be delivered and saved when we are yet in bondage? How can we claim victory in our Christian lives when we live in defeat? How can we say that we have strength when we are overcome by the circumstances of life? As Paul wrote in 2 Corinthians 4:7-10:

> But we have this treasure in jars of clay to show that this all-surpassing power is from God and not from us. We are hard pressed on every side, but not crushed; perplexed, but not in despair; persecuted, but not abandoned; struck down, but not destroyed. We always carry around in our body the death of Jesus, so that the life of Jesus may also be revealed in our body.

Do struggles negate the gospel? Does the fact that we have hardships in our lives, that we undergo stress, that crises come into our lives, make the gospel void and meaningless? Of course not! Christians have hardships just like anyone else. But the difference lies in how we deal with the hardships, how we live in the midst of hardships. That is where the ground of testimony is laid. This separates the wheat from the chaff in the church.

The hardships, problems, and tragedies do not bring the cause of Christ into disrepute. Christians who do not avail themselves of the grace of God in the midst of those times cause onlookers to see a contradiction.

Trials can serve as opportunities to manifest the supernatural power of God that enables us to keep faith and maintain hope. When we keep our commitments, we show the power of Christ and point others to the source of our faithfulness: the God who never leaves or forsakes us.

Realizing Our Potential

A third result of forsaking commitments is that, when we do not follow through, we limit our potential. My wife and I once watched a movie about a farmer whose crops wasted in the fields because his brother-in-law failed on his promise to harvest.

Facing certain ruin, the farmer took a team of workers and went out on the road to harvest other people's crops to try to make enough money to save his farm. In was an inspiring movie. There was a point in the story, however, when the farmer hit bottom. It looked as if he would lose it all. During this time, one of the workers quit. Before the boy could walk off the work site, up drove the farmer's wife with some new equipment. The day was saved! They were back in business.

The young man who had quit just minutes before came back to the boss and apologetically asked for his job back. But the farmer replied, "You know, every time you quit you get a little smaller, and before long everything looks too big."

That is the problem with quitting. The next time it gets tough, it will be that much easier to quit again. And the next time as well. Before long, it will be almost impossible to do anything without giving up. There comes a time when you have to put your head down and plow straight ahead.

This is the point Paul was trying to make about John Mark. Paul did not want to create another situation for failure to occur again.

One day, if it were imaginable, the devil decided to go out of business. Satan placed all of the tools of his trade up for sale. As the buyers looked over the assortment, they saw malice, greed, lust, hatred, prejudice, and all of Satan's arsenal at bargain prices. But one little wedge-shaped tool had an extraordinary price, more expensive than all the others put together. "Why is this little tool priced so high?" they asked. Lucifer answered, "That little instrument is called discouragement. When all the other tools fail, it *always* works."

What tool is Satan using in your life to get you to quit doing the work of the Lord? In order to achieve what we are capable of doing in life, we must persevere. There is one ability that every person can have: dependability.

Note

1. *Proclaim,* Jan.-Mar. 1987, p. 34; adapted from *Parade,* 5 Feb. 1984, p. 17.

6

When It's Hard to Know What Is Right

Voting for a political candidate can be a difficult decision. I rarely know anything about the candidates first hand but must rely on information sifted through the media. Often, none of the candidates completely satisfies my criteria. At times it is a matter of choosing between undesirable options. This kind of decision is known as choosing between "the lesser of two evils." One political analyst described the last gubernatorial election in my state as "the evil of two lessors." My sentiments exactly!

How I wish that the *only* difficult decisions in life were those made in the voting booth. Those kinds of decisions, though important, are easy to make in comparison with vocational, financial, and moral decisions which confront me on a regular basis. Sometimes it is hard for me to know the right—or the best—thing to do. When it comes to deciding my family's financial future, purchasing a home, making a move, or dealing with several options—not to mention temptations—decision making can become a preoccupation.

Every person feels the tension of decision making. It's easy for well-meaning Christians to want pat answers to complex problems. To be sure, one of the grave dangers of making important decisions is *oversimplification*. I know of a church that recently fired *all* of its staff members. This was a simple solution to their complicated problems—too simple. While such a simplistic solution may appeal to our pragmatism, it may not adequately resolve the problem. Oversimplification is like amputating a foot in order to cure an ingrown toenail!

Of course, there is also the danger of erring on the side of *overcomplicating* the matter. The lights in the sanctuary were too dim. Worshipers were having trouble reading their Bibles and hymnbooks. In general, the room had a gloomy feel to it. A committee was formed to study the problem and recommend a solution. Experts were called in. After examining lumen ratios and square footage, it was recommended that additional lighting be installed—which entailed a tremendous cost.

Finally, someone had the bright idea of asking, "It seems that the lighting used to be adequate. What's wrong with the lights we have now?" This prompted a whole new direction of investigation which revealed that the aged rheostats were not allowing full voltage to reach the lights, thus lowering the intensity. Furthermore, it was discovered that when the light bulbs were last changed, long-life bulbs were installed; these were not as bright as ordinary bulbs. After replacing the dimmers and bulbs, full light was restored at a relatively small cost.

If you found it hard to sort through the details of this brief account, that's the point! The whole issue had been overcomplicated. Often it is best to look first to the obvious solutions before embarking upon a maze of complex remedies.

I have found that these same tendencies—oversimplication and overcomplication—exist in the thinking of people concerning theological and moral issues. The rule-book approach tries to make everything fit into a black-and-white scheme where there is clearly a right and a wrong choice. Gray areas cannot be tolerated; it must be black or white. The rules make it much easier to make decisions; it is either right or wrong. In addition, it must be right or wrong in every situation, regardless of any complicating factors. Absolutes reign.

To the other extreme is the situational approach. Rules and principles should be bent to the mold of each unique situation. All is relative.

Some decisions are easily resolved. In fact, some issues are, indeed, black and white: The right thing to do is obvious. Unfortunately, this is not always the case. It may be easy to decide whether or not to commit a heinous crime but not so easy to know which vocation to choose. For example, the Bible does not give a set of rules for determining the merits of electrical engineering as opposed to computer programming as a career choice! Nevertheless, there are clear biblical guidelines for making decisions.

There are times when we are forced to choose between options that are all unpleasant to us: some may even involve some confusing moral issues. Our options at that point are to take the simplistic, rule-book approach and look for the easy answers, the situational approach wherein the decision is dictated by the situation, or to struggle with the decision. Struggling with the decision may involve tension and ambivalence: the price to pay for a decision you can live with. When making decisions, there are at least three questions to ask yourself.

What Are the Rules Involved?

Before you change the whole light fixture, try a new bulb first. If you find yourself driving against the flow, perhaps you're going down a one-way street—the wrong way! Rules are the basic building blocks of decisions. They are an essential place to start in ethical matters.

Behind any valid rule is a workable principle. Traffic laws provide for safety, order in society, and equal access to public roads. Rules are like the sheet-metal exterior of the Statue of Liberty. Without the intricate superstructure inside, the statue would blow over with the first gust of wind. Rules must have a skeleton of principles to be functional.

By examining each of the Ten Commandments, you can find an underlying base of principle for each rule. The prohibition against murder is founded upon the value of human life. One expression of this value is in the preservation of life: The Commandment in negative form—"Thou shalt not murder"—could also be expressed, "Thou shalt preserve human life." As such, the rule becomes a workable principle for guiding decision making. A simple decision to run a red light may very well violate the value of someone else's life, should an accident result.

You are driving down the road late at night in the middle of nowhere and come upon an accident. A physician and his wife have gone off the road, and the wife is seriously injured, bleeding profusely. The doctor tells you that unless he can get medicine and supplies for her in thirty minutes, she will die. There is a drugstore fifteen miles away. In order to get the medicine and supplies, you would have to drive faster than the speed limit and possibly run two red lights. In addition, you would have to break into the drugstore and steal the supplies. What would you do?

This story presents a dilemma in that you are faced with either saving a human life or violating laws. While most persons would have no difficulty deciding what to do, the dilemma does present a challenge in how one would justify his actions. Could not the speeding, running red lights, and theft result in the loss of others' lives? Suppose the rescuer has an accident in his panic mission and injures or kills someone? Suppose he is arrested or shot trying to steal the supplies? On the other hand, laws require passing motorists to stop and render aid.

On the surface, this dilemma seems to set the value of human life against rules, and even rules against rules. Actually, the story presents a principle against itself: the value of human life. This principle serves as the motivating factor for the rescue of the injured woman; it also serves as the rationale behind traffic laws. The right of private property is the principle behind the Commandment prohibiting stealing. However, the immediate probability of the woman's death without rescue serves to override the somewhat remote possibilities of personal and societal injury on the part of the rescuer. After all, with the emergency resolved, things can be set right at the drugstore in the morning. The doctor's wife could not wait that long.

Have you ever played a game with someone who changes the rules to fit the situation? What could normally be an entertaining diversion soon becomes a frustrating test of patience. What are rules, and who makes them? Webster defines a rule as "an established guide for conduct, procedure, etc.; custom." The point is that no one can make a rule on his or her own. Rule making must involve the group and requires a period of time for the rule to be recognized and assented to.

I believe that every person must follow God according to the dictates of his own conscience. I may disagree with a person's conclusions in following God in such a way, but I would fight to the death for his freedom to do so. Yet, at the same time, I recognize that the community of followers must come to some agreement on what the rules are. Therefore, it is not just an individual decision. This is the basis of society and church life as we know it today.

It would be easy to say that all Christians must follow the rules in the Bible. The problem is that the Bible is not a book of rules. The Bible contains some rules, but it is much more than a Book of divine statutes. Rather, the Bible is a Book that contains the revelation of God in history as He relates to persons.

What Are the Results of the Decision?

In a maintenance shop, one worker was using a blow torch to cut the bottom out of a barrel. Nearby stood a barrel of waste oil with a funnel in the top. Sparks from the torch spewed everywhere. Concerned about the possibility of fire, the welder asked a worker standing near the oil drum to watch the sparks. A few moments after the welder resumed cutting, the oil drum exploded. Luckily, no one was injured. "I thought I asked you to watch the sparks!" yelled the welder to his co-worker. "I did," said the man. "I watched them go right into that oil drum!"

To blindly follow supposed rules of actions, disregarding the outcome of those actions, is to invite disaster. As Paul said, "The letter kills, but the Spirit gives life" (2 Cor. 3:6).

To talk about considering the results of a decision as a part of the process is not to say that "the end justifies the means." But means that do not have regard for consequences are just as improper.

A company wants to produce a chemical solution to make a huge profit. The existence of the company is vital to the economy of the small town where it is located. Many of the residents of the town would be out of work if the company were not there. The manufacturing processes produce hazardous waste chemicals. If the company disposes of the waste chemicals as specified by law, the profits would be severely decreased. Since the profit margin is important to the management, the waste chemicals are buried in a vacant field behind the plant. Two years later, the rate of birth defects in the town's population is significantly higher than it had been before the chemical production. Chemical contaminants from the waste dump have infiltrated the aquifer serving as the community's water supply.

Here we have a fictional dilemma of competing results. The health of a community is sacrificed for the company's profits and the local economy. Is it worth it for a few children to go through life crippled or mentally handicapped in order for a company to be successful or for jobs to be secure?

We need to be careful how we follow rules. Every rule has exceptions. Some rules are bad rules. But what about the rules of the Bible? Are there exceptions to these rules? Can we follow biblical rules without regard for the consequences?

Jesus sometimes disregarded the prevailing rules of his day. For example, the law prohibited healing on the sabbath. Christ said, "It is lawful to do good on the Sabbath" (Matt. 12:12).

Jesus taught that the religious establishment had built up a set of rules supposedly based upon God's law. The whole system of man-made rules collapsed under the storm of God's judgment. Jesus could see the persons behind the principles. Can we?

What Are the Relationships Involved?

A businessman has an opportunity for a great promotion with his company, but it involves moving to another state. If he moves, his salary will almost double, the family's standard of living will rise, and they will be able to afford to send their children to the best schools. Leaving will also mean being far away from his wife's parents. The children have grown up in the neighborhood, and lifelong friendships will be broken.

In this illustration, the results are competing with relationships. Economic progress for the family is postured against cherished relationships. Will the payoff be worth it? Perhaps the new job will allow the mother to quit work and spend more time with the children. That would be a plus for the family. On the other hand, the increase in salary may require more responsibility and more hours at work. The father may have even less time to spend with his family. His present nine-to-five job may become eight to six or even seven to nine.

For the Christian, one very important relationship comes into play. It is one's relationship with God. This should clearly be the most important factor in making any decision. Because persons are concerned about what God thinks of their decisions, they tend to emphasize one thing over another. They may put all the emphasis on rules and not concern themselves with outcomes or persons. Others may emphasize relationships. Peace is bought at any cost. The rules do not matter as long as relationships remain intact. To them, all that matters is that "the loving thing" is done.

It is difficult to juggle the various issues involved in important decisions. What are the alternatives? A simplistic decision that blindly hurts people? A loving decision that throws morality to the wind?

What About the Absolutes?

What is the rock-bottom basis for morality? Why is right right and wrong wrong? From time to time, one hears preachers and teachers talk about absolutes. What do they mean?

The idea of an absolute is some standard of right and wrong that is unchanging. The line of reasoning is as follows. If God never changes, then what He commands never changes. If the unchanging

God commanded that you should not bear false witness, that will never change because God never changes.

Absolutes are bound up with the nature of God. As God is the "same yesterday and today and forever," then God's standards do not change. There's just one catch, however. Rules are not absolutes. Rules, if they are valid, are based upon principles which are based upon absolutes. The two are not the same: rules and absolutes. Rules are founded upon very basic and widely acknowledged principles of morality. But what are the underlying principles based upon? Absolutes.

What, then, are the absolutes? Historically, Christians have acknowledged two absolutes: love and justice. Love and justice are the two great ethical themes running through the Scriptures. Christian decision making is really the balancing of love and justice. *Balance* is the key word.

Absolutes never change, but what it means to live out an absolute may be different from one situation to another. The loving thing to do in one situation may be a cruel thing to do in another. The just thing to do in one situation may be the unjust thing to do in another.

One of the refreshing aspects of Jesus' teaching is the way He brought us back to the absolutes. When He was asked about divorce, he referred to God's intention for marriage in "the beginning." When Jesus gave the Sermon on the Mount, He was really giving an exposition on moral absolutes, getting to the real heart of ethical living.

The believer has the resource of the indwelling God for struggling with decisions from the broad perspective of rules, results, and relationships. With such an approach, you're not likely to stray from what is right!

7

When You Can Share Your Faith

He began attending worship services regularly on Sunday mornings. Gregarious and verbose, he would corner me after the service and talk until practically everyone else had left the building. One day he began to share some wonderful ideas. As a wealthy, eccentric, and benevolent benefactor, he wanted me to take part in a compassionate plan for the poor families in our community. I was excited as I listened to his vision. Soon I began to get letters and packages of materials from him in the mail. Before long, it all sounded too good to be true.

I was drawn into the delusions of a poor, mentally ill man. He really did believe his own delusions, but they were only a part of his fantasy world: the world as he wanted it to be. Bless his heart, for he was a man with noble ideas who was sadly out of tune with reality. He wanted to give so much, but had so little. All he could give was the illusion of blessing.

Many wish empty blessings upon others. In his essay on practical Christianity, James described such an attitude as faith without deeds.

> What good is it, my brothers, if a man claims to have faith but has no deeds? Can such faith save him? Suppose a brother or sister is without clothes and daily food. If one of you says to him, "Go, I wish you well; keep warm and well fed," but does nothing about his physical needs, what good is it? In the same way, faith by itself, if it is not accompanied by action, is dead (vv. 14-17).

Many Christians obviously wish their fellow humans well, but take little or no positive action to carry forth that wish. Perhaps they are out of touch with the reality of a faith that works. To them, faith is a warm feeling, a good intention, but it has little to do with the daily realities of life in a sophisticated, urbanized, secularized world. For this reason, Christianity has come to be something that is lived out in a closet or safely within the secure environment of a church building or church group.

The apostle Paul was a pioneer in the spiritual frontiers of first-century Roman civilization. He willingly left the Judeo-saturated world of Palestine for the hustle and bustle of many pagan cultural and economic centers: Ephesus, Corinth, and Rome. In such an environment, Paul lived out a revolutionary ideal. Self-assured in the validity of his faith, he led the avant-garde of the faith, conquering the empire with the gospel. The message of Christ had become his own. Much of the New Testament remains as the fifth gospel: the gospel according to Paul.

Until the gospel becomes *your* gospel, it remains someone else's gospel. What is the gospel according to you? What is your faith all about? Does it work? Do you back it with deeds and actions? Does it have the hard-won stamp of certification from the trials of life?

You can't give away what you don't have. If your faith is a delusion of good will or an illusion of holiness, all you can give away are empty dreams. My four-year-old daughter lives in a child's world. She goes back and forth between reality and her imaginary world at will. When she leads prayer, she thanks God for "all the people in the whole world," even though she has no concept whatsoever of the world or how many billions of people live on this planet. When she blows soap bubbles, she runs and catches them for presents to give Daddy. These kinds of thoughts and actions are the stuff of childhood. It's great, and I am constantly enthralled with her zest for the ethereal. But for full-grown, full-blown Christians, superficial prayers and empty bubble gifts aren't enough.

There Must Be an Experience

Experience is at a premium. We demand a political candidate who has the right kind of background and is a proven leader. Physicians serve a rigorous internship and residency before being allowed their own practices. Even the mechanic at the corner service station is expected to know what he is doing and have the experience necessary to perform a tune-up. Likewise, a Christian witness rings true only as it represents a life that has been to Calvary and back.

Paul's experience was as unmistakable as it was outstanding. Knocked from his mount on the road to Damascus by a blinding light, Paul had an unforgettable encounter with Jesus (Acts 9:1-19).

Though Paul's experience has trappings of the unusual in many ways, it is still normative in one crucial sense: It was a personal experience of conversion.

Evangelical Christians have long held a consensus of the necessity of this one characteristic of true Christian faith. There must be a time in the believer's life when he or she had an experience of conversion: a conscious awareness of the salvation transaction, when a person claims by faith the gift of grace and commits all to the risen Lord. It may have occurred at the altar of prayer during the invitation in a worship service, in a dark bedroom at home or in a hotel, during coffee break at work, or after school. Growing out of a childhood of Christian education and religious upbringing, a young person may come to realize that Mama's and Daddy's faith has become his own. It is a personal experience: as unique as the day that person was born; as unforgettable as that person's wedding day; and as meaningful as the sum of life itself.

When in your life did Jesus stop you in your tracks and give you a personal audience? That is your faith, your witness, your gospel. Share it.

There Must Be a Life Behind the Words

As a fellow worker lay on the floor of the shop, dying of a fatal injury, employees crowded around him as he breathed his last words: "I'm dying. Can anybody tell me how to be saved?" Silence. Afterward, a guilt-ridden layman shared with his pastor that even though he knew the "plan of salvation," he was paralyzed from witnessing during that tragic event because of his unchristian life-style as an employee.

Acts 16 holds a similar story with a very different ending. Paul and his missionary companion Silas were arrested for preaching the gospel and placed in stocks in a dark prison. That night as they sang hymns, an earthquake shook the building and rendered the prisoners free. The Roman warden of the prison, knowing he would suffer the sentence of every escaped prisoner, drew his sword on himself. Paul cried out that all prisoners were present and accounted for. The warden called for a light and rushed in before Paul and Silas with the desperate plea, "Sirs, what must I do to be saved?" (v. 30, KJV). Before dawn, the warden and his family were baptized believers!

One never knows what spiritual issues may come to the fore during a crisis in a person's life. Frank's heart was pounding as he stumbled from the crumpled wreckage of what used to be his car. Stunned and barely able to stand, he gazed at his bloodied arm and wondered how he could still be alive. Swerving to miss a motorist who ran a stop sign, Frank had lost control of his car on the state highway and crashed into a ravine. Knowing his wrecked car could have easily become a fiery coffin, he for the first time grimly faced the prospects of his own death. Later that day, he voiced his fears to his Christian roommate.

A different crisis confronted Sara. No nightmare was as bad as reality was for her now. In three swift months, cancer had stolen her husband. Alone, with staggering debts, she thought seriously of taking her own life. Grief's pain and hopelessness overwhelmed her with a mud slide of despair. Closing the medicine cabinet where she had found an old prescription of pain pills, Sara picked up a gift copy of the New Testament which she read until late in the evening. Waking the next morning, she called the church office to make an appointment with the church's counselor.

At a hospital the chaplain walked into a room to find the patient, John, gazing out the window at the cloudless sky. "Hi, I'm Chaplain Johnston. Enjoying the view?" "Actually," John listlessly replied, "there isn't much to see." John was scheduled for exploratory surgery the following morning. His anxiety spilled into his conversation with Chaplain Johnston who was able to verbalize John's feelings in prayer.

An automobile accident, the death of a loved one, and illness or hospitalization are all crises that may precipitate the awareness of a deep spiritual need. When people have questions, they go looking for answers. Will they come to you? Can they?

Why did the Philippian jailer instinctively go to Paul and Silas during his own spiritual crisis? Could it be that those songs in the night attracted the warden's attention hours before? Had he noticed something different in the way these two prisoners responded to their unjust treatment?

There Must Be Care Before You Can Share

Rosella walked into the furniture store office in response to the advertisement for a bookkeeper. Her charming personality, adequate skills, and colorful Hispanic humor more than compensated for her limited English. Within a few weeks she had adjusted to her new job and was quickly making friendships.

Helen, one of Rosella's new friends in the accounting department, expressed Christian concern when Rosella broke into tears during a midmorning break. In an outburst of frustration, Rosella recounted years of abuse from her husband and her subsequent fear and turmoil. Helen offered emotional support and a referral for counseling.

While seeing a counselor at a denominational center, Rosella began attending church with Helen. She found new vitality for her faith, which had grown dormant since she left her Central American home and church. More than a trusted friend, Helen became a spiritual sister.

Many churches in our land are floundering in the midst of intensified evangelistic emphases. Baptistry waters are rustled each week, new members respond to Sunday morning invitations, and church rolls are expanding. Yet in many cases something is missing. The statistics do not tell the whole story.

Are ministers and members alike subscribing to a mechanized method and a generalized gospel? Take a four-month course and learn to win a person to Christ in thirty minutes! Present a slick witness and a packaged presentation to the newcomers of your community! Play the salesmanship percentages: bang on enough doors and you're bound to get some results! But the results might not be lasting.

Please do not misunderstand me; I'm certainly not opposed to evangelism and discipleship programs which teach a structured presentation of the gospel. I have personally been blessed by such programs. What bothers me is the way many of these programs are employed in churches as an overzealous approach to fast numerical growth. It sometimes comes across as selling an ecclesiastical bill of goods.

The relational emphasis of the gospel should force us to read between the lines of the biblical accounts of sudden conversion. Apparently the warden of the Philippian jail was converted in an instantaneous progression of events encompassing only one evening. A longer look may reveal some deeper truths.

The warden's suicidal intentions were only the logical conclusion of a series of logical assumptions. Given half a chance, many criminals would flee. The earthquake provided such an opportunity. The law would require the soldier in charge of the prisoners to suffer their fate. Self-inflicted death would obviously be the preferred option.

Paul's cry from the dusty darkness of the dungeon signaled not only the hope that all prisoners were remarkably accounted for but the powerful influence of the gospel as well. The loving message was loud and clear: "Don't harm yourself!" In addition, the moral actions of Paul and Silas formed chains of influence which had taken each prisoner captive to the knowledge of Christ.

Are there not persons around us who seem to be locked into their logical conclusions of helplessness and hopelessness? Their plight appears unsolvable. Yet the unexpected concern of a Christian and the undiscovered power of Christ can alter the picture drastically. By framing life's problems from the perspective of faith, they take on an entirely different appearance!

Through sharing the Christian frame of reference with persons, we draw them into faith. They are then enabled to receive the grace of God and find ultimate meaning in life and assurance of hope. Such opportunities cannot be preprogrammed. We must be vigilant for the moment when the door of grace opens.

There Must Be an Understanding of the Gospel

In order to be able to capitalize upon opportunities for witness, the Christian must have the ability to articulate his or her faith. Paul's understanding of the gospel is evident in his voluminous writings which comprise the heart of Christian doctrine. I am not the first to wonder what the form of Christianity would be had not this zealous Jew been accosted by the love of God on the road to Damascus! Paul's reply to the Philippian jailer's panicky plea is one of the most succinct and inclusive statements of the gospel in all of Scripture. Then Paul and Silas "spoke the word of the Lord to him and to all the others in his house" (16:32).

What would have been your reply to the warden's question? More important than this hypothetical question is the real possibility that you will have the opportunity to share the gospel with someone who comes to you with life's greatest question.

I am grateful for the pastors who taught me *how* to share my faith and for the evangelism and discipleship programs I completed which equipped me to verbalize the gospel. Such approaches not only helped me understand the gospel but also gave me greater confidence to seize opportunities for witness. Now I am "prepared to give an answer to everyone who asks . . . the reason for the hope" that I have (1 Pet. 3:15).

I understand and share the concern of pastors and church members who shun the canned approach of many evangelism programs. But, I wonder, what means do these churches have for equipping their members with a workable knowledge of salvation doctrine? Furthermore, what programs do these churches have to encourage members to share their faith?

In the seminary I attended, all the Greek courses start with the same book in the New Testament: First John. The easiest Greek in all the Bible is found in this little book. Yet the knowledge the students applied to and gained from the study of this one book enabled us to begin the study of more difficult biblical texts. In a sense, the educational approach was "canned" in that we all learned the same basics. But we soon learned to embellish upon the basics!

A positive beginning resulted from applying such a principle to the study of witnessing. By learning a simple outline, the Christian is laying the foundation for a more mature understanding of the gospel and a more sophisticated approach to sharing. After all, the gospel really becomes good news when it is shared!

There Must Be Faith in the Holy Spirit

God saves, not humans. We carry the treasure of the gospel "in jars of clay to show that this all-surpassing power is from God and not from us" (2 Cor. 4:7). Sharing one's faith is an act of faith. Without the concomitant witness of the Spirit, our testimony is futile.

Taking a photograph is an act of faith in a chemical process that is little understood by the average person. By our clicking the shutter, the film is exposed with the image of the picture. Yet the image is *latent*. Exposed film looks no different from unexposed film. Only after we subject the film to certain chemicals does the image appear. The photographer trusts in a process he or she cannot see.

In John 3, Jesus noted that the Spirit is like the wind. He cannot be seen, except in the results of His work. The results of the Spirit's work are the changes effected in the lives of persons. This process is not always self-evident at first. The results take time to appear.

In relation to witnessing, there are two widespread and glaring evidences of a lack of faith in the ministry of the Holy Spirit.

Much Ado About Numbers

First, there is much emphasis placed upon numbers. The fallacy of a numerical approach to reporting the results of evangelism is that the real effect cannot be statistically measured. No one but God knows what is accomplished in the heart of a person when the gospel is shared.

A pastor, who was considered a dismal failure by modern standards, was reprimanded for the fact that his only convert during the entire year was a young boy. At the time, the discouraged minister had no way of knowing that the boy Robert Moffat would blaze the missionary trail to Africa and later be the inspiration for another young man to enter the mission field: David Livingstone.[1] D. L. Moody was known to say that it is better to win one soul-winner than a thousand souls.

Much Ado About Words

A lack of faith in the Holy Spirit's work can also be seen in a tendency to make much of wording and presentations. As a minister, I must confess that members have probably learned this from their preachers! How often are points pounded and bemoaned continuously from the pulpit, when a few well-chosen words would have been more effective? Do we preachers think we can compensate for a lack of supposed attentiveness on the part of our listeners or some deficit in spiritual power by increasing our volume and perspiration?

One day my wife's grandmother was stalled at a red light. As she was trying to restart her car, a frustrated motorist behind her continued to sound his horn. Finally the rude fellow jumped from his car and stamped up to her window yelling insults. The lady replied, "I'll be happy to go honk your horn if you can get my car started!" Likewise, no amount of preaching or coercing can put power in the lives of church members. Time and energy would be better spent helping persons to get their spiritual engines started!

Note

1. J. B. Fowler, *Proclaim*, Oct. 1985, p. 33.

8

When You're Lonely

Back in World War II, the enemy discovered that solitary confinement was a most effective form of punishment. By taking a prisoner and locking him in a room by himself for an extended period of time, the greatest mental pain could be inflicted. A person in solitary confinement, particularly in an enemy country, may lose hope. *Will I ever get out of here?* he may ask himself repeatedly. *Will I ever see a friendly face again?*

Thomas Wolfe, in *The Hills Beyond,* wrote, "Loneliness . . . is the central and inevitable fact of human existence."[1] In her book *Loneliness: The Untapped Resource,* Ida Nelle Hollaway defined loneliness as "a feeling of aloneness, a consciousness that no one can completely share our feelings or completely understand our thoughts."[2] Recently a counselee shared with me his definition of loneliness, "When you're stranded high and dry—alone." His definition has the feel of experience! This experience can take many different forms.

Kinds of Loneliness

Loneliness is a pain of various facets. Though all people share in the malady of loneliness, it remains an individual experience. Let's examine some of the most common forms of loneliness.

Alone Loneliness

Alone loneliness occurs when circumstances dictate that you are to be alone. You are driving in a car on a long trip by yourself. Perhaps you live alone. Widows and widowers may find loneliness a constant companion. While listening to a radio talk show, I heard the story of a lonely lady who so longed for the music of a personal voice that she stayed up late every night in order to hear a particular radio announcer sign off with the words *Good night to you.*

After my daughter was born, my wife made a brief trip back to our hometown with our newborn to visit our parents. As I watched her walk down the ramp to board the plane with our child in her arms, I had an acute attack of loneliness! I drove home alone. As I entered the house, I noticed an unfamiliar silence. Walking past my daughter's room, I was met with the aroma of baby powder. I was lonely and missed my family.

Elijah knew what it meant to be lonely, for it was a large part of his life and line of work. Elijah was God's man during a very important part of Israel's history. In 1 Kings 17, we encounter Elijah without much of an introduction:

> Now Elijah the Tishbite, from Tishbe in Gilead, said to Ahab, "As the Lord, the God of Israel, lives, whom I serve, there will be neither dew nor rain in the next few years except at my word."
>
> Then the word of the LORD came to Elijah: "Leave here, turn eastward and hide in the ravine of Kerith, east of the Jordan. You will drink from the brook, and I have ordered the ravens to feed you there" (vv. 1-4).

This was a period of being alone for Elijah: alone loneliness.

Alone-in-a-Crowd Loneliness

In this kind of loneliness, you may be with other persons but not with anyone you know or know well. This can be a most intense time of loneliness. You feel isolated and lost. In fact, the presence of many strange faces can exacerbate your feelings of isolation.

Because of his boycott of rain, Elijah was not the most popular man in Israel. Ahab called him the "troubler of Israel" (18:17). In the big showdown between Yahweh and Baal, Elijah was alone on God's side against 450 Baal prophets. In such a religiously hostile environment, Elijah no doubt felt lonely.

In John 5 we find a sick and lonely man in a crowd. A superstition attached to the spring-fed pool of Bethesda had it that the occasional bubbling up of the spring was an angel disturbing the water. The first person to enter the water after this rustling was supposed to receive healing. Consequently, the lame and sick encamped around the pool hoping for their chance. One of these persons told Jesus, "I have no one to help me into the pool when the water is stirred" (v. 7). No one was looking out for him. He had no friends among the many. Jesus bridged the chasm of the man's loneliness by restoring him to health and set before us a model of healing ministry to lonely persons.

Friendless and Forsaken Loneliness

Fortunately, not every person experiences this form of loneliness, at least not on a regular basis. Forsaken loneliness occurs when others actually withdraw from you. Though many persons may feel they have no friends, it is quite another situation to have others purposely avoid one's presence. They do not like you or want to be associated with you. You feel deserted, stranded, and forsaken.

It is like being the new kid on the block or the new student at school. You do not know anyone and may feel derided for being strange or different. The other children may look down upon you or make fun of you. The young lady who doesn't get a date to the prom feels deserted and left out.

A divorced person may feel left behind or left out. The prison inmate may feel he or she does not have a friend in the world.

A patient lay in her hospital bed in isolation; her precarious condition required that all visitors and attendants be garbed in sterile robes and masks. How separated she must have felt in such an environment! Compounding her pain, a well-meaning but misguided minister brought her the unsettling teaching that her illness was the result of her own sin and unwillingness to repent! Alone and feeling forsaken by her church, she listened attentively as I shared with her Scriptures of God's love and presence.

Forsaken loneliness seems to be the most prevalent form of loneliness in the Bible. After winning his contest with the Baal prophets, Elijah was a man on the run from the wrath of Jezebel. In that experience Elijah hit bottom: "Elijah was afraid and ran for his life. . . . he himself went a day's journey into the desert. He came to a broom tree, sat down under it and prayed that he might die. 'I have had enough, Lord,' he said. 'Take my life' " (1 Kings 19:3-4). Elijah felt totally dejected and abandoned. The world had turned against him.

The Psalms are filled with expressions of the loneliness of forsakenness. No doubt David could relate to Elijah's situation as he wrote:

> Because of all my enemies,
> I am the utter contempt of my neighbors;

> I am a dread to my friends—
>> those who see me on the street flee from me.
> I am forgotten by them as though I were dead;
>> I have become like broken pottery (Ps. 31:11-12).

This is the sound of a slandered life, one shunned by the repulsion and ostracism of others. Whether victims of malicious rumors or vindictive jealousy, lonely individuals feel like lepers as people flee from their presence and take care to not associate with them.

Could this not be the pain of those who are suffering from Acquired Immune Deficiency Syndrome? Most victims have acquired the disease as a result of a certain life-style; others, through a fault not their own. They are cast out as modern-day lepers, feared and shunned by even the church, in many cases.

> My friends and companions avoid me because of my wounds;
>> my neighbors stay far away (Ps. 38:11).

Should not Christians show the love of the Christ who healed the lepers and cleansed them of their stigma by ministering redemptively to these who suffer such physical and emotional pain?

While I was driving down a long stretch of highway, my car ran out of gas. What a helpless feeling! Scores of motorists drove by without stopping to help. One man even honked and swerved around me as if to underscore my plight. I couldn't even decide which way to walk for the closest gas station! I could identify with the psalmist as he wrote,

> Look to my right and see;
>> no one is concerned for me.
> I have no refuge;
>> no one cares for my life (Ps. 142:4).

How I would have blessed a friendly face that day!

Jesus felt keenly the ache of forsaken loneliness during His ministry and especially on the cross. Jesus bore the pain of our loneliness. That our Lord shares in our loneliness, even of the forsaken variety, grants hope.

> "A time is coming, and has come, when you will be scattered, each to his own home. You will leave me all alone. Yet I am not alone, for my Father is with me.
> "I have told you these things, so that in me you may have peace. In

this world you will have trouble. But take heart! I have overcome the world" (John 16:31-33).

Toward the end of his life, Paul felt forsaken and alone. "At my first defense, no one came to my support, but everyone deserted me. May it not be held against them. But the Lord stood at my side and gave me strength" (2 Tim. 4:16-17).

Other biblical people typify forsaken loneliness. Hagar was the abandoned and scorned handmaiden of Sarah. Modern-day Hagars need angels of mercy in their hour of desperation too. Is that the role God would have you to fill as He makes you aware of their loneliness?

The parable of the good Samaritan brings home the role of God's people as ministers to the forsaken. As we find the friendless in our path, we should bind up their emotional wounds and see them through to reintegration.

Some persons may perpetuate the process of loneliness by their abrasive personalities. People do not want to be close to them. This becomes a terrible cycle as others react to their attitude, causing them to become even more unsociable, thus intensifying their loneliness. They feel the sharp pain of loneliness, which makes their attitude about life all the more sour, driving others away. Around they go in the never-ending and downward-spiraling cycle of rejection.

Withdrawn Loneliness

Friendless loneliness occurs when people withdraw from you. Withdrawn loneliness happens when you withdraw from people. This can be a pathological kind of loneliness—to withdraw from others in a state of depression. Persons who are suicidal may withdraw from others and cut themselves off from vital relationships.

There may be many reasons one withdraws from others. A person may suffer from low self-esteem, feeling that he or she is worth nothing. Another person may withdraw because of lack of confidence and the skills to relate well with others.

Elijah withdrew in his dejection and depression. He went to dwell in a cave at Horeb where the Lord spoke to him: "What are you doing here, Elijah?" Elijah was consumed with self-pity and a martyr complex, feeling that he was the last servant the Lord had on earth.

As an interesting contrast with Elijah, Jonah also withdrew. When God told Jonah to go to Nineveh, he went to Tarsus on a fishing trip and made quite a catch! I do not know what it is like to be in a fish's stomach for three days and nights, but it must have been lonely! Having suffered enough with a sour stomach, the fish spat Jonah out on the beach, where Jonah hit the ground running for Nineveh.

Jonah's preaching mission was a huge success. However, the angry prophet withdrew outside the city wall to pout in the hot sunshine.

The Phases of Life and Loneliness

Loneliness is no respecter of persons or age. We experience loneliness the first day of our lives. When we come into this world, thrust out of the warm environment of our mother's womb into the cold world, we suddenly find ourselves on our own. With a total lacking of any context for experience, we do not even know how to frame life's questions, much less understand the answers. Though we do not remember the loneliness of our birth, or the early years of our childhood when we felt alone, we still have those feelings in our subconscious. These primal feelings come to the surface when we feel alone. Children can feel desperately alone, not really understanding what is going on in their lives, as Schreiner said: "The barb in the arrow of childhood suffering is this: its intense loneliness, its intense ignorance."[3]

During the adolescent years, one of the overriding issues of life is: Who in the world am I? This can be a time of loneliness as the teenager tries out various roles, casting himself or herself in different parts in the search for identity. Such strivings can produce superficiality. Consequently, by not really feeling secure in one's identity, one is not able to relate deeply with others. The result is loneliness.

Who can I be closely related to? is the question of the young adult who seeks to meet the need for intimacy by sharing self deeply with another person of significance. Without such intimate relationships, a young adult can become painfully lonely. A sense of identity demands relationships in which to express that identity. The success of singles ministries in many churches could be at least partly attributed to the strong need for relationships on the part of postadolescents.

During the middle years of adulthood, as a person begins to reflect on such questions as What is life all about? or What have I accomplished? a sense of urgency sets in. Life is readjusted around redefined goals. As persons change in middle age, relationships may disintegrate. Children are launched into the world, marriages may dissolve, parents are aged and pass away. Loneliness, once considered a by-product of immaturity, may become a mainstay.

The latter years of life have their own kind of loneliness. Older folk, in many ways, are more prepared to deal with loneliness than at any other age, for they have been tempered by the years. Framed by experience, loneliness becomes integrated into the fabric of life: How can I look at life differently, and share my creative insights with future generations? Yet there are facets of life which exacerbate loneliness for the senior adult. Waning health, the death of a spouse, and other factors can bring about a life-style of loneliness.

What Causes Loneliness?

The causes of loneliness can be many and multifaceted. Four major contributors to loneliness rise to the top of the list.

Existential Loneliness

Existential loneliness is anxiety about the meaninglessness of life. What is life all about? One's questionings of the meaning of life can be a precursor to loneliness. Death looms as a great unknown, a dark beyond. One feels alone in existence, and what is bothersome is the possibility that one may cease existing.

Where is God in all of this? I do not believe a person feels more lonely than when he or she feels apart from God and does not have a sense of God's presence in life.

Unavoidable Losses

The loss of a loved one who has been your companion through the years or some other circumstance can thrust one into a situation of being alone. Relationships may be lost as a result of a move, career changes, or estrangement, as well as death. Loneliness is but one component in the process of grieving over any loss.

A Superficial Way of Relating

A person may have many friends but not be close to any of them and, therefore, feel terribly alone. No one shares life with you in a significant way. In an urban setting, this is all the more common. An urbanite encounters many people whom he or she can only relate to on a shallow basis.

Lack of Social Skills

Some people draw back from engaging in a deep relationship with someone because they lack the skills or confidence needed to interact successfully with other people. Generally, this is known as being shy. Maybe the person is afraid of being hurt.

Psychologists and counselors are beginning to look at shyness not as just a personality trait but as social maladjustment, a psychosocial pathology. This is a positive step since shyness is seen as not just the way a person is but as some malfunction in a person's life socially. People who are shy do not like to be shy. I should know since I am an expert on being shy!

One of the consequences of being shy is difficulty in meeting new people and making new friends. As time goes on, life has a way of taking friends away from us. The shy person may get into a mode of not making new friends and meeting new people. This is one road that leads to Lonelyville.

Neglecting the cultivation of friendships can lead to feelings of isolation and depression. As the walls of isolation rise around the shy person, self-consciousness and preoccupation with personal reactions to others and social situations becomes stronger. One focuses on self and perceived inadequacies. Anxiety focuses upon the discomfort of relating to others. As anxiety increases, the shy person has difficulty thinking clearly and expressing what he is thinking and feeling to others. Lacking in confidence, he feels intimidated by others. Acting as a block to free expression, fear keeps him from being himself around people. He may become passive, not asserting his opinions and values to others.

Others may misunderstand the shy person and adopt erroneous views of him. The shy person may be viewed by others as unfriendly, unintelligent, or weak. Timidity results in discomfort on the part of others; therefore, the shy person is avoided, which compounds the feelings of isolation and defeat. As the shy person begins to pick up on the mistaken views of others, he may even come to believe in these false notions. Self-esteem plummets. Soon he learns to avoid social contact altogether, as much as possible. The cycle of anxiety, false perceptions, and mistaken beliefs spirals downward into a black hole of loneliness.

Assertiveness training can be invaluable to such persons. By meet-

ing regularly in support groups, shy persons can learn that it is OK
to say what they really feel and think. In fact, the more articulate one
becomes in expressing true feelings, the more comfortable others are
around him or her.

Overcoming Loneliness

How can you break out of the prison of loneliness? Perhaps you
have not experienced pathological forms of loneliness, but everyone
feels lonely at times. As Joseph Fort Newton said, "People are lonely
because they build walls instead of bridges." Here are some bridges
you can build across the chasm of your loneliness.

Make Friends with Yourself

Being alone means being with yourself. One of the painful aspects
of being alone may be the company you are forced to keep. For some,
being alone is like having to spend the weekend with someone they
really do not like. They cannot wait until the time is over so they can
get back into some diversion which allows them to escape the necessity of having to live with themselves.

What makes you feel alone? Is there something about yourself that
you find hard to accept? Some persons do not like the way they look.
Others find fault with some characteristic of their personality or
life-style.

Make friends with yourself. The way to become best friends with
yourself is to realize and understand the love of God. When Jesus died
on the cross, He was not dying for you *if.* He was simply dying *for*
you. God's love for you does not depend upon your getting your act
straight, becoming knowledgeable, or being successful. "But God
demonstrates his own love for in this: While we were still sinners,
Christ died for us" (Rom. 5:8).

In spite of all of those things that we really do not like about
ourselves and all the sin that God does not like about us, God reached
out beyond and accepted us just as we are. That is where God starts.
He takes us just as we are. We need to be able to do this with ourselves,
to know what it is like to be accepted by God and ourselves. Then we
can find that others are accepting us like we are.

Take Charge of Your Loneliness

Too many persons allow life to take over when they need to learn to take charge of life. Get a handle on loneliness by turning loneliness into solitude. One book makes a distinction between loneliness and solitude.[4] Loneliness is the pain of being alone; solitude is the glory of being alone. Solitude involves meaningful time in God's world. Find your place in creation and society.

You Are Not Alone in Your Loneliness

There are two reasons one is never really alone. First, God is always present. He shares our loneliness. "Be content with what you have, because God has said, 'Never will I leave you;/never will I forsake you' " (Heb. 13:5). The writer was in effect saying that when we have God, we have enough, for God will see that our needs are met. In John 14, Jesus told his followers that He would return in the person of the Holy Spirit "to be with you forever." Not only does Christ walk with us, but He also dwells in us. "I will not leave you as orphans," Jesus promised; "I will come to you." We are never really alone because of God's presence. We can experience God's presence when we are not around others. Furthermore, God's presence in others can provide profound meaning for Christian fellowship and worship.

The second reason one is not really alone in loneliness is that there are always other lonely persons. This is not the misery-loves-company kind of commonality, but rather the fellowship of believers in the Christian faith, each meeting the other's needs.

A certain Scripture verse often interpreted to demand church attendance is actually a statement of the importance of Christian fellowship. "Let us consider how we may spur one another on toward love and good deeds. Let us not give up meeting together, as some are in the habit of doing, but let us encourage one another—and all the more as you see the Day approaching" (Heb. 10:24-25). Why is it important for Christians to get together regularly? One reason is that during such a time ministry happens. We encourage and strengthen one another in corporate worship. If we try to go it alone in the Christian life, we miss out on the biggest blessing of the Christian life, which is the shared life in Christ. The church is a community—a family.

As we reach out to others in their loneliness, we lose ours in the process. And so do they! One of the best ways to overcome loneliness is to help someone else overcome loneliness. To find motivation for ministry to the lonely persons in the world, we should remember the pain of our own loneliness. When we hear the sound of loneliness from others, we may recognize it as a familiar sound that has come from within our own souls.

Do you know someone who is alone and possibly lonely at this moment? Perhaps today or tomorrow you will meet someone who is in a strange place among strangers. Can you break the ice of loneliness for that one?

Can you reach past the barriers that others may have erected around an ostracized soul and reclaim him or her from isolation? Are you willing to hear the angry sounds of a heart broken with denigration? Are the arms of your love long enough to reach into the shell of someone who is withdrawing? Can you break the cycle of that loneliness?

Notes

1. Thomas Wolfe, *The Hills Beyond* (New York: Harper Brothers, 1941), p. 186, cited by Ida Nelle Holloway, *Loneliness: The Untapped Resource* (Nashville: Broadman Press, 1982), p. 34.

2. Hollaway, pp. 75-76.

3. Olive Schreiner, *The Story of an African Farm,* cited in John Bartlett, *Familiar Quotations* (Boston: Little, Brown and Company, 1968).

4. Paul Tillich, *The Eternal Now* (New York: Charles Scribner's Sons, 1963).

9

When Life Is So Good that You Forget God

In the spring, at the time when kings go off to war, David sent Joab out with the king's men and the whole Israelite army. They destroyed the Ammonites and besieged Rabbah. But David remained in Jerusalem. One evening David got up from his bed and walked around on the roof of the palace. From the roof he saw a woman bathing. The woman was very beautiful (2 Sam. 11:1-2).

"Brother Mark," queried the voice on the phone, "can I see you at the church for a minute?" Wondering what Joe Carpenter had on his mind, I walked out to my car. A few minutes later, driving into the church parking lot, I saw Joe standing outside the sanctuary. *It must be important,* I thought; *he wasted no time getting there.*

As we walked into the building, Joe asked, "Remember that thunderstorm last night?" "Yes, indeed, it was a rough one." "It sure was—blew my barn to bits," Joe lamented. "I'm sorry. Anything else get damaged?" I asked. "No. But, you know, Brother Mark, I can tell when the Lord's trying to get through to me."

Joe placed a check in my hand. It was for a large sum and was written to the church. "Yeah, I figured it was about time I got things squared away between the Lord and me. Put that in the offering for me." Joe's close call with the weather had prompted a spontaneous revival of stewardship!

At my brother's ordination service, a dear pastor and friend recounted during his sermon how it was to minister during the Great Depression. "When hard times come," he said, "people turn to God. When times are good, they tend to forget Him." My own experience has served to verify the preacher's statement. Not only have I found it true in my ministry that people seem to take a keen interest in church and religion during times of crisis, but I have found it true in

my own life as well. Looking back, the times when I felt I was closest
to God were the hardest times.

David was a success. He was a popular king who extended the
military power and geographical boundaries of Israel to a zenith. Due
to his great zeal for the Lord, worship reached an unparalleled height,
as David's many psalms attest. But David's heart was prone to wan-
der when his concerns were unleashed from worry by blessings and
affluence.

Easy Street Is No Place to Grow Up

I know a man who was one of many children in a poor family. He
worked his way through graduate school by washing dishes. He was
a hard worker by nature and very conscious of the value of a dollar.
Now he enjoys the golden fruit of his long career. Like few men of
his caliber that I have known, he also maintains a strong spiritual
devotion to the Lord.

David's love for the Lord is unquestioned, for God Himself described David as a man after His own heart. However, in the luxury
of his affluence and in the security of his political power, David grew
bored. Even a challenging military campaign no longer interested
him. In the midst of mid-life crisis, David's loyalties were confused.

As much as we strive for success and affluence, these remain intan-
gible goals. While visiting in the home of family friends, I was admir-
ing their house, replete with fascinating art, fine furniture—all the
niceties of the good life. Yet during our conversation one of them
exclaimed, "I just wish we were in a little better situation financially!"
Retorting in smooth cliché, I said, "But money can't make you happy." "Oh yeah," he shot back, "then make me miserable!" Success
places its own built-in limitations on personal growth. The rewards
of success are often translated into an unhealthy life-style of indulgence and inflated desires.

Advertisements for fitness centers pepper newspapers and magazines. The ads feature models sporting shapely and finely tuned phy-
siques. The rewards of exercise are alluring. Well-conditioned bodies
not only look better but also feel better. Unfortunately, unless the
routine is rigorously maintained, the rewards soon fade. Modern man
is learning that physical exertion is a way to build the body and to
maintain health. We humans were not designed to sit at desks all day!

The August 6, 1984, issue of *Time* contained an article about

Bomber, a twenty-two-year-old eagle that was being trained to fly into the main stadium during the opening ceremonies of the Olympics. Bomber didn't make it, for he died during practice. Unaccustomed to the strains of flight, the captive eagle suffered a massive heart attack from the rigors of the rehearsal.

A life completely free of stress is a bane rather than a blessing. "Suffering produces perseverance; perseverance, character; and character, hope" (Rom. 5:3-4). If I restate Paul's formula for hope in the negative, the outcome is clear. The complete absence of stress would result in the atrophy of our endurance; the absence of endurance would rob us of moral strength; our lack of moral resolution would land us in a hopeless situation. "Therefore, prepare your minds for action; be self-controlled; set your hope fully on the grace to be given you when Jesus Christ is revealed" (1 Pet. 1:13).

A consistently developed spiritual life during the good times affords tremendous strength during the bad times. I, like many pastors, am all too familiar with "bad weather" religion. Though most people have "fair-weather friends"—persons who stick closer than a brother during prosperity and vaporize during crises—many people have a "bad-weather religion." They somehow remember God's resources when they run out of their own. When the skies of life are cloudless, they are too preoccupied with their fair-weather friends to think of the God beyond the blue. Bad-weather religion does not hold up in stormy times, like the house of faith built on the sand.

Success Often Leads to Excess

"I wish I were rich!" said the young boy to his father. "You do? How would you know when you were rich?" The boy thought for a second and then said, "When I had more than I could take care of!" Looking around the boy's disheveled room, the father concluded, "I would say you're pretty wealthy already, then!"

Material blessings have spiritual liabilities. It is not impossible for the rich man to enter heaven, Jesus taught, but it is like squeezing a clumsy camel through the small "eye of a needle" gate in the city wall. The way to the kingdom is a narrow way. The constricted requirements of righteousness leave little space for materialistic baggage. In spite of the relative wealth of our society in comparison to other countries, we are adept at thinking of others as rich. Indeed, the average American is a part of the wealthy elite of the world.

It is too easy for us to get hooked into the thinking that if we just had a bigger house, newer car, or larger salary, we would be content. And we would be . . . for a while. But as soon as our desires regained equilibrium, we would be window shopping for other items just beyond our reach. Such was David's lot.

Bored, sleepless, and dangerously successful, David was drawn by the sight of a beautiful woman performing her cleansing ritual in the cloak of darkness. She was figuratively and literally just beyond his reach. Morally and practically speaking, he would have been better off going back to bed—alone.

The more power and responsibility given to a person, the more potential exists for good and evil. The biblical historians recorded the relationship between the spiritual maturity of Israel's monarchs and the spiritual level of the nation. The king set the pace. David's love for the Lord promoted a revival of worship in the land. His sin was cause for national mourning.

Referring to David's tryst with Bathsheba as a great sin is not to say that such a sin in someone else's life would be of a lesser sort. The point is that David's sin had a great potential for damage due to his high position in government and his heroic spiritual status in the eyes of the nation. Sin's ruinous effects, however, are universal among all people. David's sin was great, for it was an audacious and gravely immoral act. The debauched nature of David's adultery was high-lighted by the murderous plot to cover it up. That David would stoop to such depths pointed out his brash disregard of the most rudimen-tary of moral standards.

Sin has its consequences, and great sins have great consequences. One result of David's sin with Bathsheba was that the sword of violence never departed from his house (2 Sam. 12:10). The sword, as a symbol of David's violent act in covering over his sin, remained as a perpetual memorial in the Davidic dynasty. David's great success soon had a fly in its ointment. Inner strife and heartache plagued his family for generations—all stemming back to this one incident. In seeking to satiate his overgrown appetite for pleasure, David had swallowed a bitter pill with foul consequences.

Success Can Make It Easy
to Forget the God Who Gave It

God's response to David's actions was swift. Through Nathan's tactful approach, the king was shown the magnitude of his sin. David stood accused by his own words and standards. Nathan reminded David of God's multitudinous blessings, which only magnified the seriousness of David's adulterous and murderous schemes.

> This is what the Lord, the God of Israel, says: "I anointed you king over Israel, and I delivered you from the hand of Saul. I gave your master's house to you, and your master's wives into your arms. I gave you the house of Israel and Judah. And if all this had been too little, I would have given you even more" (2 Sam. 12:7-8).

God's use of the first-person pronoun is obvious. "I" emphasized God, "I gave you" all that you enjoy. Such is the danger of material blessings. The blessed forgets the Blesser.

Some preachers today emphasize the difference between references to God's hand and His face. Could it be that the blessings that flow from God's hand have the effect of leading us away from His face? In the Hebrew language, *presence* is literally "in the face of." David, as a picture of every person, had become so enthralled with the benefits of God that he had lost a sense of God's presence.

Last Christmas I made a mistake. I worked long hours in my wood shop making a toy stove and sink for my little girl; it was her main request. Remembering the mystical wonder of Christmas in my childhood, I wanted my daughter to have a magical visit from Santa Claus, resplendent with wonderful gifts (a challenge on our budget).

As we came home late on Christmas Eve from family visits, we put Carli to bed. Mama witnessed her excitement when she heard the faint sound of reindeers' bells through the window (Daddy standing out in the cold waking up the neighbors with bells). The next morning found the living room filled with toys, complete with a stove and sink. Carli was ecstatic. We captured on videotape her joy.

What was the mistake? For weeks, every time someone came over, Carli would show off her new toys. Even months later, when asked who made the stove and sink, she replied, "Santa Claus did." I keep silently hoping for the day when she will be old enough to understand who Santa Claus really is!

As a father, I often wonder if my feelings are not in some way similar to my Heavenly Father's. Does He feel a tinge of regret when His children become so engrossed in the benefits of His love that they forget from whence the blessings came? Does He also long for the day when maturity will allow His children to recognize Him in His rightful place?

Toscanini was conducting the New York Symphony Orchestra in Beethoven's Ninth. It was a stirring performance. As the crowd roared its applause at the conclusion of the evening, Toscanini turned to his orchestra and shouted above the applause, "Gentlemen, you are nothing; I am nothing; but, gentlemen, Beethoven is everything!"

As God's children enjoy the blessed life given by our Savior, let us not forget the source.

> He is the image of the invisible God, the firstborn over all creation. For by him all things were created: things in heaven and on earth, visible and invisible, whether thrones or powers or rulers or authorities; all things were created by him and for him. He is before all things, and in him all things hold together. And he is the head of the body, the church; he is the beginning and the firstborn from among the dead, so that in everything he might have the supremacy (Col. 1:15-18).

10

When You Have a Sin You Don't Want to Give Up

King Solomon, however, loved many foreign women (1 Kings 11:1).

The usual light atmosphere of the weekly pastor's conference had given way to a serious spirituality as one young pastor stood to ask his ministerial brothers to pray for his weakness with lust. In a few moments, another pastor stood to share his sinful secrets. Soon the luncheon became a smorgasbord of confession as minister after minister told all. Nearly everyone present had bared his soul when all eyes focused on one squirming brother sitting near the door who had yet to speak. Sensing the attention of the expectant group, he jumped to his feet, edging nervously toward the exit, and said, "Well, my sin is gossip, and I just can't wait to get out of here and talk to somebody!"

This humorous story illustrates the sad truth that persons can be very aware of a vice in their lives—cognizant of its destructiveness—and yet be adamant in maintaining it. Franklin said, "What maintains one vice would bring up two children." Yet we gladly pay the price! The cost of sin may seem small until we add up the total price of daily indulgence, like an apparently small leak in the plumbing which at the end of the month shows up in an enormous water bill!

If you are laboring under the heavy burden of guilt over some sin, you've got a problem, and you know it. Whether you realize it or not, you're headed in the right direction just by recognizing the problem. But for those other sins, why don't you quit whatever it is you're doing that bugs everybody so much? Because it doesn't bother you, right? And since it doesn't bother you, why read about how to quit doing what you intend to keep doing? Hear me out. You wouldn't have gotten this far if you weren't a little concerned about changing your act. After all, who is on your case? Is it your kids, spouse, boss, counselor, or just that little voice inside?

Have you ever read the Book of Ecclesiastes? Have you ever wondered how the writer of that book got to be so burned out and bitter? After all, it's not exactly a Positive Mental Attitude to say, "So I hated life, because the work that is done under the sun was grievous to me. All of it is meaningless, a chasing after the wind" (2:17). The author of those words was Solomon, the glorious king of Israel. Remember him? He was the guy who had all the wisdom, money, and power. How did Solomon ever wind up in such a state? He had it all, but at the end of life he wound up a cynical old man. Ecclesiastes is the memoirs of a man sharing the tragic lessons of his own mistakes. Why? What was it that derailed his "good-life express"?

The turning point in Solomon's life is recorded in 1 Kings 11. Solomon was at the pinnacle of his glory. Solomon had asked for great wisdom, and God had granted it to him. Even in the secular world today, Solomon is known for his wisdom. But the cancer that ate the heart out of his life was a subtle spiritual disease. The great king, through many marriages of alliance with the surrounding pagan societies, had fallen prey to false religious practices.

How could such a wise man succumb to such a thing? Satan had found an inroad into his life. One may be strong in the Lord, but Satan will search out his or her weaknesses. He will find that vulnerable point. Satan, indeed, found Solomon's Achilles' heel.

Solomon's sin was not just that he had many wives. His wives were pagan. They were people of false gods, and their religions were "detestable" to the Lord. To some of these gods were offered human sacrifices. Many of these pagan religions involved Temple prostitutes. Spiritually, Solomon had hit rock bottom. He worshiped false gods and built places of worship to them. His idolatry remained in his life and overcame him. He did not want to give up his sin, which had become a dreadful spiritual disease.

How can you recognize the course of this disease and catch it in time? The cure involves three steps. First, let us look at the germs under the microscope.

Magnify the Sin

After Pasteur discovered germs, some medical doctors did not take seriously the implications of germs. They scoffed at the idea of washing their hands before performing operations! What finally convinced the medical world that germs were for real? The microscope! As the microscope came into widespread use, more doctors could see for themselves the danger of bacteria. The microscope magnified the image of germs several times to the point of being very visible.

I remember my dismay upon looking through a microscope at a drop of tap water in a junior high school science class. There before my wide eyes were all kinds of hideous-looking creatures swimming in the same water I had been drinking all my life! Another experiment proved that unseen bacteria exist in the air we breathe and can be grown in a petri dish.

The chronicler of Solomon's life did not gloss over his sin; he made a big deal out of it. The writer commented that Solomon had married many women (one thousand) from various nations from which intermarriage was forbidden by the Lord (1 Kings 11:2-3). The result was that "his wives led him astray" (v. 3). "So Solomon did evil in the eyes of the Lord," the writer concluded in verse 6, and "The Lord became angry with Solomon because his heart had turned away from the Lord, the God of Israel, who had appeared to him twice" (v. 9). In fact, the author must have been quite indignant about Solomon's sin, for he continued to emphasize it. He pointed out that even though God "had forbidden Solomon to follow other gods, Solomon did not keep the Lord's command" (v. 10).

In dealing with our own shortcomings, we tend to avoid microscopic examination. Here are three often-used tactics for diverting attention away from the significance of our spiritual mistakes.

It's Not that Big a Deal!

The natural tendency of human nature is to minimize our sin. We invent new labels for old sins. Adultery is called an affair or "something on the side." Stealing is the art of "ripping off" or "pinching" things. A lie is little more than a fib or "bending the truth." "Adult book stores" are outlets for pornography and havens of gross immorality. A partner in fornication is called a "live-in" and the act is termed "shacking up." All these terms cannot cover the terrible reality of sin.

We may minimize our sin by comparing it to "big" sins or enormous misdeeds. After all, we rationalize, it's not like embezzling a million dollars from the poor man's fund or murdering someone in cold blood.

By downplaying the sin, we hope to alleviate our misgivings about it. Furthermore, societal mores are on our side as these terms become widely used and accepted. Why do we go to such lengths to avoid the biblical terminology? Could it be that by calling sin by its proper name we would be hard pressed to avoid its evil connotations? What are you calling your sin? One important means of overcoming habitual sin is to face up to it and call it what it is.

We must use caution against adopting societal norms of morality. Society can be immoral, just as individuals can be. Just because an action may be right in the eyes of people in general, it is not necessarily right in the eyes of God. The standards for right and wrong are not the geographical location or the community in which we live or what most people believe. The Word of God is the standard, and the standard does not change because God does not change.

God Will Probably Overlook It

Just to make sure Solomon understood the serious consequences of his behavior, the Lord sent a personal message. "Since this is your attitude and you have not kept my covenant and my decrees, which I commanded you, I will most certainly tear the kingdom away from you and give it to one of your subordinates" (11:11). Perhaps Solomon had fallen into the trap of becoming comfortable with his sin, thinking God was unconcerned.

God has other things on His mind than this trite little sin, we might assume. What may seem miniscule to us may appear significant to God. Furthermore, the fact that we think of our particular moral problem at all is an indication that we have not completely overlooked it. Has God?

It Won't Hurt Anybody

A popular ethical principle many people invoke when morality is being discussed is: "If it doesn't hurt anyone, what's wrong with it? It is just something in my life, and it is not even that big a deal with me." On the surface, this appears to be a good principle. That which does no harm to others surely could not be wrong. However, the catch is that we cannot know all of the effects of sin.

Solomon may well have reasoned, *After all, what damage is my harem doing to others? Have I committed adultery? Have I murdered for my wives as my father did for Bathsheba?* But notice that God's judgment on Solomon was to tear the kingdom from the hand of his son (v. 12). The future of the dynasty was altered as a result of Solomon's sin! How can you possibly know that your sin will not affect others in the future? Sin brought misery to the house of Solomon. Can you escape its consequences?

Root Out the Sin

Solomon's sin was of two sorts: commission and omission. In verse 6 we are told, "So Solomon *did* evil in the eyes of the Lord; he *did not* follow the Lord completely, as David his father had done" (emphases mine). He did, and he did not. A sin of commission occurs when you do something wrong, whereas a sin of omission is failing to do what is good.

In *doing* evil, Solomon had a well-established practice. He had one thousand wives! One does not attain such a harem overnight. At the rate of one new wife a month, it would have taken Solomon over eighty-three years to collect them all! Solomon's sin required a great deal of activity. This was a sin which must have carried its own punishment!

Perhaps the greatest tragedy of Solomon's sin lay not in his commission of sin but in the omission: "He did not follow the Lord completely." In spite of his greatness, Solomon fell far short of his potential in life. What heights he might have reached had he not wavered in his devotion to God!

Sins of omission are often harder to kick than sins of commission, for they involve inaction. We find it harder to initiate a good practice than to stop a sinful habit. All the inactions of not helping, listening, giving, loving, encouraging, speaking out, and being involved have robbed us of the good we could have done, had we done it. "Anyone, then, who knows the good he ought to do and doesn't do it, sins" (Jas. 4:17).

Sins of omission may be hardest to forsake because they are invisible. They exist only in the missed potential for doing good. We may feel good about our lives because of all the sins we do not commit. But what about the good we fail to do?

Dealing with sin is like pulling weeds: If you just pull off the tops, they will grow back—you must dig them up by the roots. I know a man who struggles to resist the temptation to buy and read pornography. For months he frequented an adult book store on the way to work. He lived with the secret shame of hiding the materials from his wife and children. So strong was his habit that often, without thinking, he would stop at the book store. The more he resisted his desires the stronger they became, and the guilt mounted. Finally, through group therapy, he was able to bridle his sin, for it was a force which he was powerless to face alone.

The roots of sin may run deep into our hearts. Though we excuse our actions as mere behavior gone awry, from whence comes the behavior? What drives us to sin again and again? What is the real problem?

Settle the Deeper Issue: Lordship

In verse 4, the root of Solomon's problem is revealed: "His heart was not fully devoted to the Lord his God, as the heart of David his father had been." Although David was not perfect and had his own moral failings, the Scripture attests that he was a man after the heart of God. David's heart was in the right place, though his eyes sometimes wandered! His highest joy in life was the worship of God. Solomon's heart was not in the right place; his spiritual loyalties had been divided. The statement in the Scripture literally means that Solomon was not at peace with God. Furthermore, he was living in disobedience to God. Solomon's problem was centered in his loyalty; he was not fully submitted to God's lordship.

Immoral action and moral inaction are only symptoms of a deeper problem in life: the issue of lordship. Who or what is in control of your life? Whom are you serving? It is futile to wrestle with the trappings of sinful behavior until the one central issue of life is settled.

I am not saying that if you simply confess the lordship of Christ, all your sin problems will go away. I am saying that it is useless to try to effect a change of behavior until there has been a change of heart. If you have the courage, look to the source of your behavior and ask if your heart is in the right place. Having a sin you do not want to give up may only indicate that you are not willing to abdicate the rule of your life to Christ. As Jesus said:

> "If you hold to my teaching, you are really my disciples. Then you will know the truth, and the truth will set you free. . . . I tell you the truth, everyone who sins is a slave to sin. Now a slave has no permanent place in the family, but a son belongs to it forever. So if the Son sets you free, you will be free indeed" (John 8:31-36).

11

When Life Gets You Down

How do you know when life is getting you down? When you realize that all the parts in the airliner you're flying on were supplied by the lowest bidder! Life can get you down when you tell the dentist he just pulled the wrong tooth, and he says, "Don't worry, I'll get to it!" You know life is getting you down when the only way you can get up in the morning with a smile on your face is to have gone to bed with a clothes hanger in your mouth. You know life is getting your wife down when she is so nervous that she can thread the needle of her sewing machine while it is running![1]

Were it not for a healthy sense of humor, life would be unbearable at times. A columnist in a local newspaper has an affinity for writing humorous anecdotes about ministers. On three occasions he has recorded the hilarity of my chagrin. He has been able to transform embarrassment into amusement, such as the time my deacons forgot to invite me to a dinner they were having for my birthday!

One particularly distressful evening revealed a humorous side when described in the writer's article. My wife had cooked all day to provide supper for a young couple in the church who had just had their first baby. I was in a rush to deliver the meal and return to the church for visitation, and my rough driving landed the whole meal in the floorboard of my pickup! Vincent van Gogh could not have portrayed a more dejected expression than the one on my face as I delivered hamburgers to the hungry family instead of casseroles!

Aside from these trite examples of temporary exasperation, how can one cope with life when things look hopeless? How do you handle the pressure cooker of frustration when you are stressed beyond your limits and do not even have a safety valve to let off the steam? Where is the sunshine in your cloudy gloom and despair as depression sets in like a dark fog? When cracks appear in the foundation of your sanity, what assurances do you have that termites of doubt aren't eating away at your faith as well? Have you ever felt that you were living in the basement of life instead of the penthouse and that you would be content to just make it to ground level?

Jesus has good news for those whom life is getting down: "Come to me, all you who are weary and burdened, and I will give you rest. Take my yoke upon you and learn from me, for I am gentle and humble in heart, and you will find rest for your souls. For my yoke is easy and my burden is light" (Matt. 11:28-30). Christ was speaking to those who were oppressed by the unbearable burden of the "yoke" of the law. The phrase was a familiar one to first-century Jews. The rabbis spoke of moral and legal obligations as "the yoke of the kingdom of heaven," "the yoke of the Commandment," "the yoke of the Holy One," "the yoke of heaven," "the yoke of God," "the yoke of earthly government," and "the yoke of earthly conduct." It is easy to see why Jesus said that the teachers of the Law and the Pharisees "tie up heavy loads and put them on men's shoulders, but they themselves are not willing to lift a finger to move them" (Matt. 23:4). Religion was a burden no one could successfully carry, with its unbearable moral regulations and codes. The pharisaic traditions were used to oppress and put down the masses who could not live by them rather than to teach the way of joy and faith.

A yoke is an obligation that one submits to. The problem is that a yoke can become a noose—a killing, oppressive stricture—that chokes life. Persons may submit to certain yokes in hope of fulfillment, joy, and pleasure only to find that these yokes become the chains of slavery and the gallows of death. "Don't you know that when you offer yourselves to someone to obey him as slaves, you are slaves to the one whom you obey—whether you are slaves to sin, which leads to death, or to obedience, which leads to righteousness?" (Rom. 6:16).

There is the yoke of alcohol and other drugs: addictive tyrants. What begins as social enjoyment and a release from stress soon can become a nightmare of unimaginable miseries. The yoke of fornication has entrapped many in the dungeons of sexual addiction or sexually transmitted diseases. The yoke of materialism binds its victims in the ropes of debt and financial bondage. There are the yokes of fear, depression, poor self-image, and loneliness.

Jesus' words in Matthew 11:28-30 are like an emancipation proclamation to weary souls toiling under yokes of burden. He offers relief and fulfillment.

Do you feel that life is getting the best of you rather than you getting the best of life? If so, it is time to stop and make some evaluations.

It's Time to Examine the Cargo

Imagine you are a bellhop in a busy hotel. Guests are hurriedly placing pieces of luggage at your feet and calling out their room numbers. As you struggle to carry every bag possible—probably breaking the world's record as well as your back—you are met by another customer. He asks, "Tired of carrying all that luggage?" "Yeah!" you whisper between hard breaths. "Then carry mine!" comes the reply. If he means to carry his bag *in addition to* the others, he is being nothing but sadistically cruel. However, if he means, "Carry mine *instead of* the others," your customer is offering a blessing. "I only have one small case," he says, "and I'll pay you more than all the other customers combined. Besides, my bag has two handles— I'll even help you carry it!"

Jesus' offer may sound strange at first. He gets your attention by saying, "Come to me, all you who are weary and burdened, and I will give you rest." Sounds good. But then He says, "Take my yoke upon you." What? Come to Christ with your burdens, so He can place another burden on you? Sounds ludicrous!

What Jesus means is to exchange burdens. "Take *my* yoke upon you" (author's italics). Exchange one yoke for another, change the yoke of the world for His yoke. Jesus is not promising an escape from the trials and struggles of life, but He is promising to give the Living Power with which to face them. Every person needs a yoke, a burden to bear, if he or she wishes to have joy and fulfillment. After all, what is fulfillment but to be filled full!

A couple of years ago I was vacationing in Corpus Christi, Texas, on the Gulf Coast. While enjoying a scenic boat ride of the bay area, I took a picture of a huge cargo ship sitting empty at dock. What drew my interest to this particular ship was a large round hole in the bow, or forward part. As we sailed past the ship I could see that the hole went clear through and that a propeller was inside. The tour guide explained that this propeller was to help the captain navigate the big ship through the shipping channels. When the vessel was fully loaded, the propeller was under water. I noticed a gauge on the side of the ship which is used to determine the depth of the vessel in the water. The more cargo aboard, the lower the ship lay in the sea. In order for the ship to be able to navigate properly, there had to be a certain amount of cargo aboard. Too little cargo—or too much—and the ship would not be seaworthy.

The word Jesus used for *burdened* literally means "ladened," as a boat overladened with cargo. It is the same word Paul used in Acts 27:10 to describe the cargo on his boat that sank in a storm. Christ appeals to those whose cargo holds are dangerously full. Your ship is about to capsize on the stormy waters of life. However, Jesus offers not to completely alleviate your load but to replace it with one more suitable. "My burden is light," He says.

Often I hear persons complain about having stress in their lives. Actually, we would be terribly unhappy without *any* stress! Stress is not bad in itself, though too much stress can be detrimental to health. What we need is an optimum level of stress, or motivation.

A '67 Chevy pickup I once owned did not ride well until there was a load in the back. The PA system at my church can be damaged if turned on without someone having hooked up the speakers. The amplifier is designed to operate under the resistance or "load" of the speakers. We all need a certain amount of stress to keep us going. Without it, life would really be dull. On the other hand, too much stress can warp our perspective, making everything look negative.

I knew a man who committed suicide. He was a successful professional and well respected in his community and church. His untimely death was tragic. Why did he kill himself? My best guess is that he could not bear the burdens of his success. He excelled in everything he did, but it was too much for him.

Life can load us down with some terribly heavy burdens. Even the burdens of our success—the added weight of our accomplished goals —can create an unmanageable stress. If life is getting you down, it is not time to throw in the towel and dump all your burdens. It is time to examine the cargo and see whose load you are carrying.

When the moving van arrived at our address, I was in for a new experience. My new employer was paying all the expenses for packing and transport. All I had to do was supervise! As the movers opened the doors of the van, I was dismayed to see that it was already half full of someone else's goods. "How can you get all of our stuff on that truck with someone else's stuff?" I asked. "We've already loaded two other households on the truck; you're the third," they said. To my amazement, all my earthly goods fit in the remainder of that van!

People are not like moving vans. We cannot carry all of our stuff (concerns, responsibilities, and stressors) and someone else's at the same time. "No one can serve two masters. Either he will hate the one and love the other, or he will be devoted to the one and despise the other" (Matt. 6:24). Whose load are you carrying? Everyone serves someone.

Are you serving yourself? Many modern thinkers teach us to center our lives around ourselves. "Be in control of your own life; chart your own destiny." Advertisements encourage us to indulge ourselves. "Buy something just for you." But is being the monarch of our own little kingdom really what it is cracked up to be? Listen to the words of such a king:

> I thought in my heart, "Come now, I will test you with pleasure to find out what is good." But that also proved to be meaningless. "Laughter," I said, "is foolish. And what does pleasure accomplish?" I tried cheering myself with wine, and embracing folly—my mind still guiding me with wisdom. I wanted to see what was worthwhile for men to do under heaven during the few days of their lives (Eccl. 2:1-3).

In his search for self-centered fulfillment, Solomon built himself houses with beautiful landscapes, acquired a small army of servants, amassed a huge fortune, collected fine art of all kinds, embraced a large harem of beautiful women of all nations, and attained a golden reputation as Israel's greatest king:

> I denied myself nothing my eyes desired;
>   I refused my heart no pleasure.
> My heart took delight in all my work,
>   and this was the reward for all my labor.
> Yet when I surveyed all that my hands had done
>   and what I had toiled to achieve,
> everything was meaningless, a chasing after the wind;
>   nothing was gained under the sun (Eccl. 2:10-11).

In describing the ruinous end of false teachers, Peter characterized them as "those who indulge the flesh in its corrupt desires and despise authority. Daring, self-willed, they do not tremble" (2 Pet. 2:10, NASB). The burden of a self-serving life is too much to bear. We were not created to serve ourselves but to serve God. Jesus offers weary self-servants a reprieve from the slave bondage of egocentricity. As Paul discovered true selfhood in the service of Christ, "I have been crucified with Christ and I no longer live, but Christ lives in me. The life I live in the body, I live by faith in the Son of God, who loved me and gave himself for me" (Gal. 2:20).

Every great person has served a great purpose outside of herself or himself. Yet, in order to overcome self-centeredness, one must be in control of self. To serve Christ, to champion a noble cause, to selflessly invest life in the progress of high principles—each of these requires a volitional decision to channel one's life toward these goals. To not be in control of your life is to be out of control—to be controlled by those forces outside you. For Christ to be in control of your life, He must control from within you—as you choose to follow Him and focus your life around this spiritual center.

Are you serving sin? Jesus said that "everyone who sins is a slave to sin" (John 8:34). Sinful action sets up its own perpetuating, self-defeating cycle.

My first full-time job was at a barrel manufacturing company the summer after I graduated from high school. In the plant I worked at different stations in the process of making fiber drums. The plant was half factory and half warehouse where thousands of various-sized drums were stored. One day while helping to stack a load of small drums, I made an error. Trying to place a stack of about ten little drums on top of another stack, I let the tall stack tip over. Making no effort to steady the stack, I backed away thinking it would be easier to just pick up the few falling drums and start over. But a chain reaction was immediately set into motion. Soon a roar filled the warehouse as hundreds and hundreds of little drums came crashing into a heap! I spent the rest of the day undoing my one little mistake!

The overload of your life may be the result of sin's vicious cycle. Like the codependent who divorces one alcoholic spouse only to marry another or the abused child who grows up to abuse his children, patterns of self-defeating attitudes and behaviors may cast a long shadow down the road of your life. The compounded interest of one sinful investment can be staggering!

It is important that we discover the cycles of our sin so that the yoke may be broken. By turning from old life-styles, thought patterns, and habitual practices, we can trade in the old yoke of sin for the new yoke of upright living. "Let us throw off everything that hinders and the sin that so easily entangles, and let us run with perseverance the race marked out for us. Let us fix our eyes on Jesus, the author and perfecter of our faith" (Heb. 12:1-2).

Are you serving God? This may be a simplistic question, for views of God differ. What kind of God are you serving? Some bear the yoke of a vindictive God who lashes them at every turn, prodding them on in fearful submission.

Jesus said that his yoke is easy and light, for He is "gentle and humble in heart" (Matt. 11:29). To truly discover that God is gracious and loving may be one of the greatest reliefs in life! Our Lord wants us to have a blessed and joyful life. He has our best interests at heart. Is He the God you are serving?

It's Time to Unload

It was her first vacation. As we loaded the car for the long trip, she walked up to me with an armload of favorite stuffed toys and games. "Darling," I said to my three-year-old, "we can't take all of these. You'll have to decide which one you want to take. The others will have to stay home." "But Daddy, I want to take them all!"

Life presents us with dilemmas at times. Hard decisions must be made between what we want and what we want most. By attempting too much, hanging on to too many options, or bearing the burden of too many anxieties, we may soon find ourselves burned out and used up, cashing in vitality as life gets us down! The question is very simple to state, though hard to answer: What is most important to you?

Just as a ship needs a certain amount of cargo to be seaworthy, so too much cargo can overdo it. We must realize that we are not unsinkable. When you find yourself up to your neck in water, it's time to unload some things!

It's Time to Unload When You've Got the Wrong Cargo

A few years ago a huge barge off the East Coast was loaded with garbage for transport to a dumping ground. Once it was loaded, however, the owners could find no port to accept their cargo! For weeks, the barge, with tons of stinking trash, sat anchored at sea.

Have you ever felt that you have something in your life that you do not want, and no one else wants either? As a pastor of an urban church in a large city, I had people come to my office almost every week with problems no one else wanted to hear. Transients, down-and-outers, out-of-luckers, and in-a-jammers—each with a dilemma which only a few bucks could alleviate—made their pleas of crisis: I need a place to stay. We're out of gas. I don't have any food to eat. My landlord is evicting me. The baby is sick. My husband left me. The gospel mission is full. County welfare will take two weeks, and I need help now. The church down the street said you could help me.

These persons wanted quick fixes for a life-style of problems, and everyone was turning a deaf ear to them. Somewhere down the line they got on the wrong track, and they've been lost ever since.

A young woman had gotten herself into a tragic predicament. She came to worship one Sunday, as a last-ditch effort to find answers. Her alcoholism and sexual promiscuity had driven away her husband. The courts took her children and assessed her with child payments. She was lonely, working hard to pay her debts, and living only to see her children every other weekend. She was in a real mess! She had turned to the only One who could help her with a problem she could not stand to have but was powerless to rid herself of.

Christ has the power. He can break the yoke of transgression (Lam. 1:14).

In one of Aesop's fables, a donkey loaded with heavy bags of salt slipped from a narrow bridge and fell into a river. As the running water dissolved the salt, the donkey was delighted to find that his load had been washed away. On the next day, while crossing the same bridge, the donkey decided to repeat his accident and purposely fell into the river. Dismayed that his load was now infinitely heavier, the donkey had not noticed that on this day his cargo was sponges!

Sin is a cargo that will get anyone down. Paul exhorted Christians to "put off your old self, which is being corrupted by its deceitful desires, . . . and to put on the new self, created to be like God in true righteousness and holiness" (Eph. 4:22-24). This is possible because of the burden-bearing ministry of Christ. "Surely he took up our infirmities and carried our sorrows" (Isa. 53:4).

Paul enunciated a pivotal principle for life change. In order to rid ourselves of spiritually cancerous cargo, we must replace it with good. Jesus described the situation of a person delivered from an evil spirit in which the demon returned to find "the house unoccupied, swept clean and put in order. Then it goes and takes with it seven other spirits more wicked than itself, and they go in and live there. And the final condition of that man is worse than the first" (Matt. 12:43-45). To put off sin without replacing it with good is to invite greater calamity. Our ships must be filled. If we put off the old, we must put on the new. Exchange the old yoke for the new yoke of Christ.

A woman used to relating to others through intimidation and threat found herself without many friends. Her abrasive personality alienated most persons around her and short-circuited her deepest desire for intimacy. Frustration and self-condemnation flooded forth as she related her pain to a friend. Realizing the vicious and perpetuating cycle of her pattern of relating was a good start. Yet learning new and more appropriate ways of relating to others was a formidable task. She found it easy to lapse into the old patterns when confronted with threatening situations. Only after learning a new set of relational skills was she able to discard her old dysfunctional ways.

It's Time to Unload When You're Overloaded

Supermom was supertired. Cleaning house in the wake of her family's daily acts of domestic terrorism was getting to be too much. Empty clothes lay like casualties on the floor, their dirty shapes still retaining semihuman form. Dirty dishes were scattered like debris on the kitchen table. Bloodstains—no, just catsup—spotted the floor. Newspapers camouflaged the den. A limb—perhaps still attached to a body—protruded from the easy chair clasping the television remote control. Sounds of battle emanated from the screen as grown men in brightly colored uniforms fought tirelessly over a small leather object. Never mind the fact that Mother-maid had to go to work in the morning.

Every boat has its capacity—its limits. What is your breaking point? How much added stress does it take to capsize your ship? A twelve-foot sailboat cannot possibly carry as much as a cargo ship, and a frigate cannot sail the local reservoir. We must know our limitations. God does.

"We have this treasure in jars of clay," said Paul (2 Cor. 4:7). Is your pot cracking under the strain of the "treasure"? Has your sweet wine turned to vinegar? Are you killing yourself in the process of trying to live by unrealistic expectations? It's time to unload.

"How can I unload?" you protest. "No one else will do it!" Sure, no one else will do it—as long as you are doing it!

Back in the seventies, the big fad was the discovery of one's spiritual gifts. I found mine: administration and service. Actually, I'm not sure whether these are gifts or liabilities. Administration is the ability to see what needs to be done and see that it gets done. Service, however, is the ability, or desire, to *do* what needs to be done. Every administrator needs servants to carry out the planned tasks. Every servant needs an administrator. My problem was that I was both! Not only did I see the needs and plan the tasks, but I did the work. The church members loved it! I mowed the grass, lit the furnace, opened and closed the building, and performed countless other chores in addition to my pastoral duties. Soon everyone had spare time on their hands because all the tasks they had been doing were in my hands! Only when I unloaded did the load get spread around for all to participate. And only then could I do *my* job well.

I understand your problem. You cannot stand to let things go undone. So you do them yourself. Soon you're doing your share and everyone else's. The answer? Unload! Quit trying to carry the world on your shoulders! Who are you to assume responsibility for everyone's irresponsibility? Why do you feel you must control the uncontrollable?

I'm going to do something dangerous. I'm going to question your intentions. Do you enjoy the game? "What game?" The game you play every time you capsize your boat. There is just something about the strokes you get when you overdo it and sink like a rock.

Such a tactic meets two needs. First, it is an expression of passive-aggression, the need to get back at those you do not feel you can afford to get back at. Like the bookkeeper who "accidentally" leaves the office lights on every evening to run up the electric bill for his grouchy boss, you have guilt feelings that will not allow you to express your frustrations openly and directly. So you find an indirect route of revenge. All the while you can smile in their faces as your catastrophe causes them great inconvenience.

Second, the swan dive gets the attention you so desire. Friends and family come to the rescue as you go under for the third time. Temporarily it is all right to be inactive, and others make failing attempts to pick up the chores you find so necessary. Of course, no one can do it quite to your specifications. As soon as the crisis is over everyone goes back to normal, including you. Not having dealt with the real issues, you go back to the same old overresponsible and self-defeating behavior. Only this time you have renewed zest and affirmation.

You've gotten out some of your resentments and received the recognition you deserve. You feel better. The pattern, however, remains.

How can you possibly break out of such a pattern? By purposefully admitting your overgrown need for control and learning to give others the freedom to be irresponsible. By stopping your self-nagging, you can break out of the doing it—griping about it—and doing-it-anyway cycle. Fortunately, life provides its own incentive.

It's Time to Unload When the Storm Comes

During frontier days the desert regions of our land were littered with abandoned goods. As pioneers in covered wagons trekked across the wilderness, furniture and other valued possessions had to be left behind at certain hard crossings in order to lighten the load. No doubt, many a tearful eye looked back at heirlooms left for waste as the journey continued. Surely the rugged air was filled with arguments over what was most important to whom.

A crisis is a breaking point, a crossroad in life's paths when things can no longer remain the same. I believe that one reason God allows trials to come into our lives is to assist us in getting our priorities straight. Crises force us to decide what is really important, or we stall at the juncture. Hard decisions corner us into choosing family, integrity, or health over lesser treasures. Sometimes it is necessary to cast off good things in order to retain that which is best.

A missionary to the Caribbean once described to me an experience he had while sailing abroad. While resting on the ship's deck, he was astonished to see members of the crew throwing huge bundles of bananas overboard. Appalled at the apparent waste of provisions, the missionary questioned the captain. The captain explained that a small bunch of bananas had been found to be ripe. If left unattended, all the cargo of green bananas would ripen and rot before the ship ever docked. Therefore, the bananas surrounding the small, ripened bunch had to be discarded to salvage the whole lot.

In order to save life's best, we must sometimes jettison some good things. Projects of a worthwhile nature, worthy causes, attractive opportunities, and even warm relationships may fall short of the line separating what is best from what is, therefore, unnecessary. When crises come, only that which is absolutely necessary do we dare hold on to. All else must wait on the dock for our next voyage. As the next morning's sun rises on a cloudless day, we then find that Providence has dealt us a helping hand in finding the freedom we need to grow.

Note

1. A sampling of the humor of Tal D. Bonham's *Another Treasury of Clean Jokes*—good therapy when life is getting me down (Nashville: Broadman Press, 1983).

12

When You Really Blow It

A trusted friend has proven to be disloyal. The sting of disappointment and hurt rises like a welt on your heart. You feel a wide gamut of emotions ranging from anger to fear. You feel justified in your indignation and want to lash out in hostility. You fear, however, that others, too, may hurt you. Up go your defenses.

How you respond to the failings of others may indicate how you respond to your own shortcomings. Embarrassment, disgust, condemnation, sympathy, outrage, remorse, and anger are but a few of the reactions noted on the part of persons to the moral failures of others. How would you react? How do you respond to persons you feel have failed you?

Persons may react to the spiritual tumbles of others out of their own sense of guilt. Those who are most vocal in their condemnation of immorality in others may suffer their greatest temptations and failures in that same area. Perhaps the loudest denunciations come from those who have not escaped the consequences of their sin and feel that others should not go free either. Every person has the capacity to fail. Too often we exercise that option.

The way we react to the sins of others also reflects our beliefs about how God reacts to our sins. If you operate on the principle that every time you stump your spiritual toe or skin your spiritual knees God laughs at you or gets angry with you and sets out to get you, you will probably respond to the failures of others in much the same way. We tend to live out our concept of God.

On the other hand, if you worship and trust a living God who is gracious, generous, loving, patient, and forgiving, you will tend to manifest the character of Christ in much the same way in dealing with others. How we understand God's forgiveness when we blow it influences our attitude toward fellow sinners.

121

Scripture is replete with examples of men and women who blew it. One person who seems to have had the knack for blowing it in a spectacular way was Simon Peter. Peter had a way of setting himself up for a fall. He is the perfect storybook character, for he sets the stage for his fiascos with overblown self-confidence and assertions. The twenty-second chapter of Luke provides a fitting example as Jesus said:

> "Simon, Simon, Satan has asked to sift you as wheat. But I have prayed for you, Simon, that your faith may not fail. And when you have turned back, strengthen your brothers."
> But he replied, "Lord, I am ready to go with you to prison and to death."
> Jesus answered, "I tell you, Peter, before the rooster crows today, you will deny three times that you know me" (vv. 31-34).

Later in the same chapter, Scripture records the fulfillment of Jesus' prediction.

Fortunately, Peter's denials did not end the story. Jesus graciously restored Peter in one of the greatest accounts of divine restoration in all the Bible. After His resurrection, Jesus made a special visit to His disciples on the shores of Galilee early one morning:

> When they had finished eating, Jesus said to Simon Peter, "Simon son of John, do you truly love me more than these?"
> "Yes, Lord," he said, "you know that I love you."
> Jesus said, "Feed my lambs."
> Again Jesus said, "Simon son of John, do you truly love me?"
> He answered, "Yes, Lord, you know that I love you."
> Jesus said, "Take care of my sheep."
> The third time he said to him, "Simon son of John, do you love me?"
> Peter was hurt because Jesus asked him the third time, "Do you love me?" he said, "Lord, you know all things; you know that I love you."
> Jesus said, "Feed my sheep" (John 21:15-19).

God Still Loves You
Even When You Really Blow It

The surprising thing about the story is not that Peter denied Christ. Peter had shown himself to be impulsive, speaking when he should have remained silent and acting impetuously. After all, how many people had tried to walk on water! In spite of Peter's confident pledge of support, we are left to doubt his ability to stand behind his words.

That Jesus, knowing He would be betrayed and denied, was willing to go to the cross is the real paradox. Human blunders are not nearly as astonishing as God's matchless love.

Some aspects of the conversation between Jesus and Peter at Galilee are lost in translation. With an emphasis on the distinction between the two words for love in the passage, a whole new meaning arises. First Jesus asked Peter if he had self-sacrificing devotion for Him. Peter replied that he had warm affection for Christ. The same question was repeated the second time, with the same response. But the third time, Jesus used Peter's words, Do you have warm affection for me? This accounts for Peter's grief over the third question. Not only had Jesus accommodated Peter's lower form of love, but also the three questions were an obvious counterpart to Peter's three denials.

Peter would not use Jesus' word for love, for he felt he had failed to show such high love to his master. His actions betrayed any profession of loyalty and devotion. Yet Jesus was merciful in allowing Peter to profess his love for Christ anew.

God's love for you is not based upon how faithful you are to Him, but on His faithfulness to you. At best, your love is imperfect. You cannot love God as highly as He loves you. His love does inspire us to love beyond our capacity, for "We love [Him] because he first loved us" (1 John 4:19).

When you really blow it, God's love is more than an added source of guilt. It becomes the power to rise above both guilt and substandard actions.

It is important for us to affirm our love to others when they blow it. Children can grow up with overbearing guilt if they feel their misdeeds can somehow sour the affections of their parents. Parents should be able to say to their children, "I love you even when you misbehave." After all, is not this how we all want our Heavenly Father to affirm us?

When You Really Blow It
God Affirms Your Good Intentions

Peter had a good heart. He was not plotting evil against Jesus. Christ affirmed Peter's good intentions. Peter had stated his willingness to follow Christ to prison and death. "I tell you," Jesus told Peter, "when you were younger you dressed yourself and went where you wanted; but when you are old you will stretch out your hands, and someone else will dress you and lead you where you do not want to go." "Jesus said this," confirmed the gospel writer, "to indicate the kind of death by which Peter would glorify God" (John 21:18-19). Legend has it that Peter also died by crucifixion.

Good intentions can make us blind to the complexities of a situation. Good people, supporting what they felt were good causes out of good intentions, do not necessarily use good means.

Have you ever made a mess of things and felt that others were unable to see the good intentions in your heart? Even at our best, we still botch things up from time to time. It's the nature of the world we live in. It's one of the frustrations of our fallible nature. Yet in spite of our blundering ineptitude, God still sees our good intentions. "The Lord does not look at the things man looks at. Man looks at the outward appearance, but the Lord looks at the heart" (1 Sam. 16:7).

With the assurance that God knows our hearts and affirms the goodness that resides within us, we can face more openly the misunderstandings of others. God's power to vindicate the right and to honor our attitudes gives us hope that things will ultimately work out for the good. In addition, as we rest in God's acceptance of our good, we can deal honestly with our immaturities. In the climate of loving regard which faith provides, real growth in wisdom and integrity can occur.

God Heals the Wounds of Our Guilt When We Really Blow It

Imagine how Peter must have felt. Instead of the encouraging nod or pat on the back from Christ for his daring assertion of loyalty that Peter expected, he received a stinging rebuke: "Peter, rather than stand by Me this evening, you will deny me three times!" (author's paraphrase). Even before the words of rebuke were spoken, Christ had planted the seed for Peter's restoration. "I have prayed for you, Simon, that your faith may not fail. And when you have turned back, strengthen your brothers" (Luke 22:32).

It must have been an evening of high drama. Soldiers came; disciples deserted. Peter followed Christ at a distance—out of the picture, out of control. Before morning came, the rooster cockily announced Peter's defeat. The big fisherman was devastated and "wept bitterly" (Luke 22:62).

Peter was in the swells of dismay and depression following the resurrection. Christ's victory over death only compounded Peter's guilt and sense of failure. He had been unable to share in Christ's glorious vindication. "I'm going fishing," Peter told the other disciples, and they responded, "We're going with you."

Had Peter given up on the life of discipleship? Did he feel like an utter failure with guilt throbbing in his chest? Was he returning to the only life he knew outside of Christ? Years before, Jesus had called Peter from the nets to follow Him. The force of the original language suggests that Peter's leaving the nets was tantamount to forsaking the old vocation to become a "fisher of men." Though he had been a leader in the avant-garde of the new revolution, he was now a disillusioned net tender. Peter's faith had run aground.

Guilt can serve as a self-fulfilling prophecy. When guilt overruns its banks and floods our lives with self-condemning declarations, we may heed its insistent voice. Frank Minirth and Paul Meier in their book *Happiness Is a Choice* described how guilt can cause depression. Guilt, or anger toward self, arises from failure. As the anger is internalized, depression results, setting up further failure, resulting in compounded guilt. Persons locked into this downward spiral of failure-guilt-anger-depression-failure are doomed to perpetuate their guilt through further failures.

Peter serves as an instructive example of this process. Peter's failure on the night of Jesus' arrest set him up for an eventual forsaking of discipleship. Jesus was able to break the cycle by lovingly restoring Peter and reinstating his place of service. "Follow me!" was Jesus' conclusion to the matter (John 21:19).

David expressed his guilt and sorrow over his sin with Bathsheba in Psalm 51. A part of the consequence of David's sin and guilt was the depression and psychophysiological symptoms described in verse 8, "Let me hear joy and gladness;/let the bones you have crushed rejoice."

Guilt and depression can produce any number of a host of psychophysiological disorders affecting respiratory, cardiovascular, blood and lymphatic, gastrointestinal, genital-urinary, endocrine, and musculoskeletal systems, as well as the skin and sensory organs. Virtually every aspect of our physical nature is subject to the dysfunctional influences of psychological and spiritual maladies. Though by no means a cause, emotional/psychological factors have been found to affect the course of such diseases as multiple sclerosis, pneumonia, cancer, tuberculosis, and even the common cold. For those suffering under the pall of guilt and depression, God's forgiveness offers healing and restoration.

After You Have Really Blown It
God Allows a Return to Reality

Peter was crushed. One would search in vain for a biblical person who typified disillusionment more vividly. The source of Peter's confusion at least in part was his dashed hopes about Jesus as Messiah. Until the end Peter had steadfastly clung to a false notion of what the Messiah was to do. Jesus' teachings confused him, for Jesus did not fit the predetermined popular role. When Jesus tried to explain His death and resurrection to His disciples, Peter had rebuked Christ, to which Jesus replied, "Get behind me, Satan!" (RSV).

On that last evening with Jesus, Peter drew his sword to defend his Messiah. But Jesus bid him put away his sword and healed the wound Peter had inflicted upon the high priest's servant. Quite possibly, Peter's subsequent denials of Jesus grew out of his disillusionment that Jesus had so passively surrendered to his enemies. Jesus' arrest and crucifixion decimated Peter's faith with a tidal wave of confusion and disappointment.

Henry Sloane Coffin has said that we would never be disillusioned if we had no illusions. Peter's illusions had been toppled, not reality. Before he could gain a true picture of reality, his illusions had to be utterly dispelled. The cross had a dispelling effect which left Peter stunned and in shock, with no framework upon which to categorize the pieces of his new reality.

Sometimes confusion must occur before we become receptive to new ways of thinking. Persons are more susceptible to novel perspectives when their beliefs are shaken. That is a high price to pay for awareness!

When we really blow it, our confidence and understanding of self is shattered. "How could I do such a thing?" We must, however, gain a realistic view of self before we can truly begin to assume responsibility for who we are and what we do. As long as we view our actions as unrelated to who we are, we have not acknowledged our true selves. We must own our actions as unmistakable commentary on our identities and natures. But our actions are not the last word, for we can grow beyond our failures.

Perhaps the hardest lesson of all when facing our mistakes is the realization that things can never be the same again. You must come to embrace reality as it now is, not as it once was or as you would like for it to be.

The reality of Peter's failures shattered the mirror of his self-perception. Left with only fragments of who he was and the way things had been, Peter was faced with the dreadful reality that his relationship with Christ could never be the same. What he did not realize at first was that this was a most positive turn of events. For until he could see Christ through different eyes, Peter would never truly see the real Christ.

As you face the prospects of life-as-it-now-is, you may have a terribly uncomfortable feeling that life never was what it seemed to be. Are you able to abide by the new reality? Can you accept the new you, which is really the same old self that you never were able to see before? Can the reality of your imperfection lead you to grasp the newfound reality of God's love and forgiveness? That is a reality worth coming to.

When You Really Blow It
God Is Able to Restore His Purpose

Peter had been crushed and crippled by his sin and failures. Jesus came to restore Peter. With each affirmation of Peter's love, Jesus enunciated the central call of Peter's life: "Feed my sheep."

R. Earl Allen recounted this story of restoration from an A. J. Cronin novel:

He was found to have diphtheria, and a tube was inserted in his throat. A nurse was posted to watch by his bedside all night. During the night she fell asleep and awoke to find the child choking. A young woman and new on the job, she lost control and became hysterical. When they had quieted her and the doctor had arrived, the child was dead.

The doctor was furious. He filled out a report on her, noting her error. "Don't you have anything to say? Don't you know that you have just flunked nurse's training?" She stood before him, trembling, and said, "The only thing I have to say is that I want another chance. I want another chance."

Still angry, the doctor told her it was over, sealed his report, and went home to try to sleep. But as he fought for sleep, he began to ask himself the question, "Who am I to play God and to judge?" He recognized the scar that had been left on the life of the young woman and realized that she would have to deal with the tragedy all her life. He tore up the report. "In my old age," he said, "it gives me comfort to know that young woman is now head of the largest hospital in England."[1]

Like the young nurse in the story, your purpose in life is still being fulfilled. This purpose is made clearer as a result of the failures God has helped you overcome by faith—the beginning of joy.

Note

1. R. Earl Allen, *Jesus Loves Me* (Nashville: Broadman Press, 1979), pp. 33-34.